BODY ASCENSION SERIES BOOK TWO:

WAKING THE GODDESS

Angela Ditch

Book Design Angela Ditch

Cover Design by Sachia Kron and Angela Ditch

Angela Ditch c/o Zero Point Perspectives
angela@zeropointperspectives.com

The information in this book is intended to inform, entertain and inspire. It is not intended to diagnose, treat or replace proper medical, spiritual or practice based guidance. The publisher and author assume no responsibility for results of a person exploring practices as detailed herein. The experiences detailed herein are derived from the author's recollection of memorable experiences. Names, incidents, places and circumstances may have been changed or altered to protect the privacy of individuals involved.

Zero Point Perspectives Books are available through Ingram Press, and available for order through Ingram Press Catalogues.

Printed in the United States of America
Zero Point Perspectives

ISBN: 978-1-62747-088-9
Ebook ISBN: 978-1-62747-089-6

Waking the Goddess
~ Advance Reviews

"We are in a time on this planet where everyone seems to be called to find their Twin Flame, but very few people have any idea of what it's actually going to be like when it happens. There are many ways a Twin Flame Relationship can turn out, and within these pages is a very real depiction of the debilitating pain and suffering Twins must go through before their ego death on the other side of surrender. It is not a fairy tale, and that's what makes it perfect.

Angela brilliantly connects the mathematic, scientific, energetic and metaphysical explanations of how this type of union creates a zero point energy in which the masculine and the feminine collapse in on themselves creating a synergistic transmutation of karma that assists in the transformation of the entire planet. Never have I read a more detailed description of the process from start to finish.

As one of the top Twin Flame experts in the world, I can humbly say that Angela's insights on this type of union have taught me volumes thanks to her unique and vast fields of expertise as well as the clarity of her channel. This bestseller is mandatory reading for everyone looking for his or her Twin.

Waking The Goddess is the "Eat, Pray, Love" of the Twin Flame generation."

~ Ben and Jen Rode of Explosive Sexual Healing, www.eshealing.com

---

"Fifty Shades of Transparent"

"Nothing needs healing more desperately in the human psyche than sexuality. This aspect of human development has been twisted, corrupted and mutilated to the point that healthy sexual power cannot be recognized or in many cases even attained. Until now.

In an honest and open book, this brave woman lays bare her journey to uncover the truth of that incredible part of who she is, and discovers the ultimate sexual experience. She does this both conceptually and experientially through the connection of other brave souls.

Angela's insights are just what is needed to encourage the sexual re-evolution required to heal the collective soul of the thousands of years of misconceptions we have held about sexual power."

~ Tanis McRae B.Ed Intuitive Teacher/Healer

"WOW! Talk about the incredible journey of self-discovery and having the love and courage to share it! THANK YOU! I bow to you, sweet Angel, you are one amazing Goddess!

You write so eloquently and you truly have a wonderful way with words...what a "LOVE" story - titillating, spine tingling, heart warming, brave, and encouraging. You have a very full and interesting life, and have experienced many remarkable adventures. With being so raw, real and open, it has helped me look at my own life and remember to truly honor my Divine Feminine. Yes to "Waking the Goddess".

~ Shauna Cepela

To bare oneself so completely - revealing a truth to and of themselves - hidden beneath layers of lifetimes and experiences - to share it with the world for all to see - is a true testament of a healer.

Using your truth and experiences, you have shone a light on something so completely raw and human, that there is no doubt you are here to be the "Brave One".

Many of us here on earth having this human experience are hiding behind masks and layers, denying what it is we really are. With your book, you stood in front of us all, removing your masks and layers revealing a human - body - spirit - experience - and time. You stood in front of the mirror so we could see a reflection and truth in and of ourselves. Let the Healing begin! What a gift it is to experience this "humanism", to expand to the depths of who we are, what we need and why there is a strong desire for connection.

Thank you for trusting us with Waking the Goddess. Your Story, Your Truth, Your Healing and Your Expansion. For this is why we breathe.

~ Paula Gerlitz, Intuitive Healer

Dedicated to the Divine Masculine …

May the pulse of our beings .. echo out into the universe .. creating a Garden of Eden .. into which we may smile into each other's eyes .. and enjoy reflections of pure loving union ... and may you awaken in the reflection of the Goddess.

Sat Nam Beautiful Souls

Introduction

Welcome to Book Two of the *Body Ascension Series.* When I embarked on the project to scribe these books, I had a basic idea of what they were to be about. The series name and the titles were downloaded to me over, and just following, the 2012 Christmas shift. As book two wound to completion, a deeper realization of what this process meant came into my awareness.

Book One: *Avatar Anatomy* is an integration of the beginning stages of my life. Stages of learning to perceive myself from the perspective of true self, rather than body-mind. Within book one's pages, I learned to get in my body and feel safe in the world, as I stepped out on a global journey of self-realization and exploration of modality.

Book Two: *Waking the Goddess* has been a whole different experience. For within the pages of writing this book, I realized that I am not writing the book, the book is writing my life. Because the information is disseminated through the details of my life, specific experiences were needed for me to understand the scope of the message that wanted to be shared. I had no idea what I had signed up for. I am truly humbled and blown away.

This is the most raw and vulnerable experience of sharing that I could ever imagine in this moment. Thank you for being witness to this experience and holding a container of space for the words unfold before you.

Thank you for opening your heart and mind to consider another aspect of the *Body Ascension* lens.

My wish is that the words upon these pages inspire you to the courage to be your truest most divine self, burning through any fears or illusions that stand between you and the truest of divine unions – union with your true self.

~ Humbly and gratefully,
Angela

Chapter 1

I sat on the hotel room floor of the Days Inn in West Sedona, Arizona. Papers were spread across the floor as a cascade of multicolored post-it notes hung upon the wall in front of me. I was looking at the contents of my first book's manuscript in forensic detail. It was January 2013, and I had just completed Tom Bird's workshop, "Write Your Bestselling Book in a Weekend."

The method was super simple, and, after spending three days with Tom and a group of experienced writers, I now had 35,000 words of something in front of me. The trick I was having was seeing the book from one end to the other. Holding the entire thread of it in my mind was the challenge. I let my left brain go to work and attempt to organize its flow. This produced a full-printed copy, now separated and labeled with headers, while sticky notes captured the main points. I began to sequence the flow with some form of logic and continuity.

The hotel room was perfect. I had been staying with my dear friends Daniel and Silviya, but this revision process really needed a full sequestering of my attention, so I checked into this hotel and was pleasantly surprised to find such spaciousness and comfort within its walls. It was perfect.

As I sorted the categories into an order that felt logical, I came to the full realization that I wasn't looking at one book; I was looking at a minimum of three. Then my phone rang, and Tom Bird cheerfully greeted me with the question, "How are your books coming, Angela?"

He knew. He knew there was more than one in what I had begun. He had no idea of the content, but he could energetically tap into the flow of the book and feel its progress.

I laughed, explained that my realization had just been landed moments prior, and then surrendered a deadline for completion. It now required more time of gestation to birth the fully formed series. Besides, I was two days away from my next psychological cliff adventure, and that would be all consuming.

I ended the call with Tom, and, as my hand laid the phone upon the carpet beside me, a full awareness of what I was about to do two days from then came rushing into my conscious mind. I burst out laughing. I laughed so hard that tears streamed down my face and my belly began to hurt from the contractions. It seemed absurd. What the hell had I signed up for, and how did I get to this moment before consciously realizing it?

A few weeks prior, I had opened Safari on my MacBook, and onto the Facebook newsfeed I went. At the top of the page was a video link posted by one of my friends. Every cell in my body stood at attention, and the resounding sound of "uh-huh" echoed through my field. I didn't actually know what I was looking at yet, but I had already said yes.

"Explosive Sexual Healing" was the heading on the video. It was an interview done by Private Matters Internet TV with Ben and Jen Rode of Northern California. All my attention was drawn right in. I popped the video up on the screen and began to watch a very gentle couple explain the nature of their work in a professional and matter-of-fact manner.

Ben is a hypnotherapist and Sexological Bodyworker trained in Berkeley, California. Jen is a clairvoyant and Reiki Master Teacher.

Together they worked with women to open their channels of pleasure and creativity through the release of stuck energies in the G-spot and second chakra region of the body. They did this through the stimulation of the G-spot, bringing women to full orgasm and sustaining them there for up to thirty minutes. Yes! Seriously! Thirty minutes!

During the release fuelled by G-spot orgasm, women would clear trauma and blocks held in the body and experience female ejaculation.

The G-spot is basically the back of the clitoris. The clitoris is the pencil-head-like tip near the urethra. This body part travels backward over the pubic bone and is rooted in a spongy-like tissue of the vaginal cavity that produces the secretions found in the vagina. The spongy tissue is said to be the part of the sexual organ system that holds the majority of the sexual experiences and contracted energies. By stimulating this area during heightened arousal, a woman can experience full ejaculation and release of what is held in the tissues.

As I watched the interview, my mind was stuck on the repeating words of "thirty-minute orgasm." Surely, if I could be put into a state of orgasm for thirty whole minutes, by experts, I would release whatever might be left in this area of my body. And, if I could actually do this, surely, I would be healed and wide open in this area of my life and more.

I had already done a lot of work to clear the second chakra. Through intense and deep yogic practices focusing on the sacral center, I had brought the breath and energy vibrations into the area for release of repressed experiences and fears. I had reprogrammed belief patterns about sex and sexual relationships and had freed a rather torn mind from the binds of the "good girl" who longed to be the "bad girl."

I was a very sexually stimulated woman held captive by a repressive mind. I had done great work to free much of her. Surely, the explosive sexual healing would get it all.

Beyond the scope of pure sexual enjoyment and freedom is the flow of the energy itself. Sexual and creative energy are really one and the same, just as anger is also part of that same passionate fuel that moves through us in its attempts to create and express in 3-D form. If I did this work, surely, the creativity and magic would flow unimpeded.

Root and sacral chakras are keys in the manifestation of our lives. If I were to open the flow and finally let go completely, perhaps the urge to hold back, the urge to control, and the fear of what letting go might be like would finally be gone. I realized I had already signed up. This would be my very next cliff.

I love a psychological cliff. Daring to jump is the quickest way to break through the comfort zone's membrane to embody a whole new world of existence. It forces the mind to be fully present and deal with the unknown, burning through the uncomfortable as you launch yourself over its edge into an experience of no return.

I had gotten very good at witnessing my own mind. I could sit in the neutral space and just listen to the voices of the negative and positive minds and all their little aspects as they deliberated and discussed their reactions to incoming stimulus. I didn't have to react; I could just watch and learn how they operated. As this awareness came up, I had the opportunity to repattern my chosen reaction by responding in a new way and releasing the old way completely. It is how I live my life now—consciously watch and choose.

Every psychological cliff is a chance to move through a pattern causing stress or discomfort. Letting go fully in my body, and especially in orgasm, was something my mind had struggled with. I experienced orgasm, but often, conflicting thoughts and insecurities would challenge me and create tension in my body that I would have to overcome. I wanted to fully release that pattern.

Mostly, I knew that if I were to be a person who is purely authentic and in truth, I would need to relax into everything, and sexual and creative expression was the core of it all. This was my ultimate psychological cliff, and I was saying yes.

A couple of e-mails to Ben and Jen, and I was completing an intake form and picking dates. I felt like I knew these people, and, beyond the scope of the professional experience I was about to have, I also knew that at some point, we would cocreate in some way. All this knowing simply came in. It just landed. I had absolute, full, and complete trust in them. They are truly authentic people.

A forty-minute phone conversation between Ben and I got us both excited about working together, now seeing completely that we had the same intentions in our work. To bring the expanded self fully into the body to express with authenticity and full purpose was the root of everything we did.

I continued on with my writing efforts as flights and hotel bookings came together and the weeks passed by. I would sometimes imagine the benefits of what might come, still fully knowing that I had no real idea of what the other side of this experience would bring me.

Now I was sitting in the Days Inn Hotel room on the floor, coming into the full, vivid realization of the vulnerability I was about to experience in just two short days. I was about to let perfect strangers put me into a state of orgasm for up to thirty minutes. I laughed and laughed and laughed. It seemed the only way I could release the sudden fear rippling through the depths of my cells. My flight was booked, hotel was booked, and the sessions were already paid for. Holy shit! Holy, holy shit!

Chapter 2

Two days later, my truck rolled down I17 to Phoenix to catch my flight to Oakland, California. Ben and Jen were located near Berkeley in a small area called Emeryville, right outside of San Francisco. Here was yet another plane and another flight out of Sky Harbor International Airport. I love this airport.

Flying in and out of Phoenix always meant a journey to or from Sedona. Sedona is one of my true homes, and I have been blessed to have spent almost six months in each of the past six years immersing in her transformative energies and growing into a community that opens their hearts to me upon every return.

From the first time I had arrived into the Sky Harbor Airport in 2007—through the journeys to and from Egypt, Kauai, Mexico, Costa Rica, Peru, and Canada—to this very moment, it served as a transfer station and touchstone that measured my growth and transformation. I wrote for hours into scribblers on benches and carpets as I waited to board my flights. I love airports. I love flying, and the longer the flight, the better.

As we touched down in Oakland and stepped into the terminal, a humid blanket of warm air immediately touched my skin, absorbing directly into its desert-dried pores. It felt really good. All climates have their attributes, and there was nothing like the softening moisture of the ocean air.

My taxi escorted me to the hotel, and I nestled into my room that Sunday afternoon to just relax and center myself. I was a little nervous but mostly comfortably led by my inner self.

For my whole life, I had the verbal guidance of the little voice in my head. She would give me random suggestions that would assist me in day-to-day happenings, and, if I was really responsive, she would guide me to magic and profound inner discovery. Most of my life, I masked her or ignored her, or simply wasn't quiet enough to hear her. But the last many years, I moved upon her guidance only. I walked in full trust, never being let down. My life had become an epic adventure of true self-discovery.

The final page in Book One of the *Body Ascension Series* had me in January 2011 in Costa Rica, in a hammock, fully reflecting on what I had learned to that point of my journey. Now here I was, two years later, looking back upon a continued trail of adventure and discovery. I had no idea what was to come. I typically never did, but somewhere deep inside, there was always the knowing—a heightened attention poised and ready to savor every delicious morsel of the feast of wisdom about to be tasted. I was excited. I was nervous. And my true self had somehow anesthetized my little mind into coming along willingly. I still laugh thinking about how she got me there. Can you even imagine?

I began to journal all of my feelings into the computer. I had so much hope for the outcome, and yet I had a lot of apprehension for how I would deal with all that sexual energy once fully released, unconfined, and uncontrolled. My mind was really afraid of what it would be like to let go. Would I actually hold together mentally, or would it take me to a place where I could not cope? Losing control had always been my ultimate fear.

The next day, I taxied over to Ben and Jen's place. My mind, now well trained to know that high self was in charge and determined to make the jump, simply followed obediently like a child trained to be seen and not heard. As I placed my hand on the doorknob, a sense of bravery filled me with such recognition for what I had already accomplished in my evolution. Just to be able to put my hand on that very door was huge. I smiled with an even bigger sense of purpose and conviction. This was big. This was really big.

I knocked, entered, and the magic started. Within seconds of entering, the energy within my body and field was vibrating at such a high rate that any shred of doubt in being there had been replaced with a full and gentle surrender to the moment.

We all connected instantly, eyes meeting in the I-know-you-and-I-get-you kind of recognition. I felt so happy and safe to be there. I knew this would be profound, and we had only just met.

Tea was served, and then Jen started with a card reading. She had pulled three cards for me before I arrived to look at energy and subject areas at play for me that day. The cards were encouraging and succinct in their meaning. Then Ben went through describing in detail what would transpire for us in the two sessions we had planned for this day.

After all the explanation and checking in with me to see how I felt, I jumped up on the massage table fully clothed, and we began with energy work. Ben laid his hands upon my back and began to connect to me through breath and touch, taking tension out of muscles and getting me used to the feel of his hands on my body. Jen moved energy through Reiki methods and read the energies as she listened to the guidance coming through from both our teams of etheric helpers. We all remarked at how full the room felt with energy and how happy our guides seemed to be that we were all together. We knew that in some way, we would be working together. It was just a matter of time.

I kept breathing and releasing and feeling the gratitude for the fact that the universe had brought me to yet another profound experience of challenge and illumination. All the while, I watched my mind and body as it held onto deeper contractions of fear and apprehension. The gratitude waves kept lifting me above the deeper layers of the fear beneath them, encouraging me like a good coach. We were all just getting comfortable with one another as a deeper more intimate level of trust was developing.

At one point, Ben placed a special set of eyeglasses onto my head and provided me with ear buds to listen to sounds. Light emitted from the lenses of the glasses, and through my closed eyelids, I watched color dance across my internal movie screen. The sounds triggered brain-wave responses, and I began to feel more and more deeply relaxed as levels of dopamine were increased in my brain from the stimulus. I liked it very much. It was peaceful.

Jen began to speak to me about issues that were arising, in particular, the current conflict that was happening between me and my ex-partner. We had kept some joint financial obligations and were now having challenges concluding them. It was weighing heavily on my heart, and Jen could see how this and all my remaining cords to him were causing me grief. She remarked that I had somehow very nicely and neatly packed all my anger toward him and the situation into a pretty little box, like a beautifully wrapped present, and had set it in the middle of my heart. Neat and tidy and contained, but not released.

I could feel this. She gave me instructions on how to write this out for release. She encouraged me to simply let all the anger out onto paper and then burn it. I could feel the literal cords Jen found being pulled out by her skillful hands, and vast spaces of expansion were left in their place. Sometimes my guides would tell her to get me to fill the space with something, and in that would come that familiar blue, sparkly, white light that I had once expanded into several years before. This light was the entire universal field of connection. It healed. It soothed. It held an open space for pure love.

After about an hour and a half, we concluded, and they invited me to return a few hours later when we would begin the first of the three ESH sessions. I was relaxed, excited, yet still nervous on a deeper cellular level.

The taxi picked me up on Ben and Jen's curb, and back to the hotel I went. Along the way, I tried to imagine what it would have taken me to get there if I had not had the luxury of my yogic preparation. How would I have gotten to the door, let alone put my hand on the knob and enter? I had already moved past so many things for this to be possible.

Chapter 3

It wasn't so many years ago when simply being in a room where a sexually toned joke was being told would force me to suddenly need an exit, as my face reddened with my internal discomfort. I was so shy around this subject and had so much feeling of shame. A deep internal conflict around the subject of sex brewed with no conscious knowing as to what was really the root of it. The result made me a very early bloomer fascinated by the sensual urges my body had to explore.

I was twelve when a boy kissed me the first time. I liked it. I liked the mesmerizing feeling of getting lost in the experience. I felt warm and happy and completely present even though I could never have used those words to describe it at the time. In fact, I had to convince myself that it was happening to me, rather than me choosing it, because I knew that my mom would be very unhappy with me if she knew what I was doing. The subject of sex was completely taboo in my house.

It's true. For whatever reason, my mother never even told me how babies were born. I knew because I picked up the information on the street from friends at school and pieces I put together from conversations I overheard.

Then, one day, I remember being really sad about something a boy had done to me. I liked him though he didn't like me. But I couldn't tell anyone at home. Instead, when questioned about my tears, I just blurted out that everyone at school knew how babies were born but me. Groan! I was disgusted with myself the minute the words came out, but it worked. My mom was off my back, and, a few days later, a beautifully illustrated book on how babies were born was on my bed. I still have it. It's very precious.

I also remember my first orgasm. Again, I was twelve. I was in the river valley ravine near the house we lived in, kissing this incredibly popular guy from school. He was one year older and had been kept back a year, and, at thirteen, he was a prize athlete in our school. The kissing led to touching, and the touching escalated over several times of being together. This time he slid his hand down my pants and began to stroke my clitoris. I was wet and slippery, and it felt really good as our mouths continued to explore each other in such a deep focus.

All of the sudden, my body began to contract and waves of deep rolling sensation flooded from my vagina up my body. *What the hell was happening?* I thought. It scared me. What had we done? I didn't even know what an orgasm was, let alone that I was having one. I had no idea about any of it.

I pulled his hand from pants and quickly made an excuse to go home. I could think of nothing else the whole walk. The experience had both terrified me and made yearn for more. I was twelve and had no one I felt I could talk to about any of it.

Back in my hotel room in California, the alarm on my phone signaled me to stop my reminiscing and catch a cab back to Ben and Jen's for my afternoon session, my first of the Explosive Sexual Healing experiences.

My first cab ride that morning was from a basic yellow cab with a very friendly driver. Despite calling the same number, this time a black town car arrived with a driver in a suit. This was the first in many little signs that the energies were going to shift all around me.

My hand turned the same doorknob, and I walked back into the cozy space, now very warm from the heat of a small fireplace. I could smell the scent of a smudge, and the room felt clear and neutral. It felt safe.

Ben and Jen sat waiting, and they invited me to share where my feelings and thoughts were at in that moment. We were about to embark on a very vulnerable journey together, and they took every care to ensure I felt completely in control of my own process.

Ben reviewed the Stop process. He wanted me to say "stop" periodically throughout the session to retrain my inner mind to feel that she could ask for what she wanted, rather than surrendering her power over to an outside force. I would say "stop," and then when ready, I could invite Ben to begin again.

I undressed and climbed upon the massage table facedown. A soft sheet covered my body, and the two of them began to move the energy through Reiki and physical massage. Ben worked oils into my skin as he helped to relax my muscles and get me used to his touch. Soon the sheet was gone, and my naked body lay exposed and vulnerable. I was pretty relaxed to a great depth, but deeper inside was a contraction and fear.

In this practice, absolutely every program and idea that the mind holds about sex and sexual relationships comes right to the surface, and, in my awareness, I could hear a little voice of a younger version of me whisper, *"Are you sure this is okay?"*

She was worried we would get into trouble. She was so innocent and sweet, less than five years old for sure. I was reaching parts of myself I had long since buried. I was shaking at the core while my whole divine essence stood smiling with such love.

Here I was, naked on a massage table, being touched in a sensual arousing way by a man whose wife was right beside me. No, this was not like making love. This man and this couple were not my lovers. They were society, power and authority, the collective consciousness, and they were holding space for me to fully explore a potential release of all the held ideas and false programs laid from years of experience and impressions.

Not only did I have to become comfortable being so exposed, I had to work through the idea that a couple could hold this kind of session for me. It was all at once. Everything was coming up. Everything!

As the sensation began to feel pleasurable, I felt a wave of guilt. Was it okay that I enjoyed this? I could see my mother's face looking seriously disappointed in my actions, fully believing her point of view that this was very bad.

As the push and pull of mind continued, I watched, keeping as much of my awareness as possible in the body, right at the exact point Ben's hands were touching me. I knew in my yogic practice that the observation of this process was exactly what was needed in order to get to where we were heading. I needed to fully surrender, and that would mean taking layers of armor off, layers of mind-contracted ideas and beliefs that were held right in the very tissues of the body. Things I may not even know were there.

Ben had me roll over onto my back and began to work the front of my body. His hands moved across every square inch of me and began to work the insides of my legs, spreading my knees out into a butterfly position. Then he reminded me of the Stop exercise.

I didn't want him to stop, but more so, I didn't want to ask him to start again. But I obeyed his request, and the words "please stop" came from my lips. That first utterance to invite him to begin again was difficult.

At first, sound didn't seem to come from my lips at all. If I were to ask him to start, it would mean that I was admitting I wanted this sensation, and all my programming from a child had me needing the experience to be one that was happening "to me," rather than me choosing it. Even though my adult years had taught me to cope with this, the base programming still rose. "If I had no responsibility for choosing, then I couldn't be blamed" was the pattern that had been established.

The core program in my psyche was that sex was bad. The truth was that I really wanted and craved the experience of sexual stimulation. Even though I had already done much to reprogram this, every remnant of history was coming to the surface to be seen. Nothing would remain hidden. We were going to get it all.

As the full realization of my stuttering words became clear to me, I spoke louder and with force. "Please begin again," I said.

Ben continued to stroke the insides of my legs. Jen was moving energy, and I could once again feel energy cords being pulled from my body.

Ben spoke in a commanding and reassuring voice as he used the affirmations we had created together over and over to bring me back into alignment with my overall intentions for these sessions. These were statements about things I wanted to manifest in my life, and we were going to free the energy needed for the creations to flow into form. These were the details of how I wanted to fully express myself in this life.

I wanted to truly show up and teach authenticity, so more people could feel the increasing freedom of being their true selves. I wanted the books that were begging to be written to have wings to reach everyone who could benefit from their messages. I wanted to travel and continuously experience new levels of my comfort zones. I wanted to attract a beautiful soul to merge with at depths that would embody pure bliss.

I loved the way this couple interacted. They were so professional and supportive, and yet clearly facilitating a session. There was never a blur or an invitation to connect with them more deeply than in this context. This kept me firmly in my own experience and not taken down a road of manipulation, which is always a factor that one needs to consider before becoming so vulnerable. We were being connected in a way that celebrated our mutual intention for full embodiment and self-realization and nothing more.

Both Ben and Jen were very encouraging, telling me repeatedly how good I was doing, how surrendered I was, how delightful it was to hold space for me. Still inside was a layer of contraction, deep against the skeletal pathways, where the muscles were contracted. Ben saw my discomfort and knew exactly what to do when he suddenly, and enthusiastically said, "I'm getting the gloves. I'm going in!"

It worked. I burst out laughing, which broke the internal tension. Ben was like this tall superhero about to dash into a phone booth, ready to emerge as the hero of the day. I could not shake the image of him in a shiny red cape sliding latex gloves onto his hands while a sparkle of light gleamed off his smile.

Moments later, his fingers began to stroke my clitoris and slide deep into my body. My mind was so quiet it would have heard a pin drop in the house next door. I followed the sensations his fingers created and watched with my internal mind as a holographic image was created from the sensations inside my body.

My G-spot area was firm, and it was a bit ridged on the right side. It was ridged in a kind of way that reminded me of the inside of my cheek when I would wake from a night of clenching it with my teeth.

The stroking and pressure was being applied to the G-spot itself. The G-spot is specifically located in the vagina on the wall of the front body. It is a spongy-like tissue located just in front of the cervix where the body curves. Ben's fingers were creating a sensation, but the sensation was neither painful nor pleasurable. It was just a sensation. I relaxed into it as my yogic mind locked into full mode.

From the time I had left Costa Rica in 2011 to this time, I had taught kundalini yoga while I continued my exploration of deeper practices and trainings. I had become very adept at holding space for any process going on within me and around me. My mind would sit in pure neutrality while all that arose was allowed to be experienced and released. I kicked right back into this stance as a barrage of sensation and little voices filled the experience.

I felt excited. I felt shameful. I felt ugly. I felt radiant. I heard my mother. I heard my ex-partner. I heard my true self.

Scenes of memories and impressions began to rise like the time my mother walked into the bathroom while I was bathing. I was just a little girl standing in the tub with a margarine bucket in my hands. I was pouring water out across my groin, feeling the sensations of it move across my body. She walked in unannounced and simply yelled, "Angela!" with pure disgust on her face. I stopped touching that part of my body that day for quite a while. I was really little.

My mom is a good woman. I have no idea what training and indoctrination she experienced that created such a shame-based outlook around human sexuality. I know that my mother did the very best she knew how in raising six kids from a sense of responsibility that was unwavering. She thought she was teaching me well. She meant no harm. My adult self clearly understood this, but the little girl in the tub simply felt ashamed.

Ben was carefully and consciously stimulating the area to create sensations in the body, and this was effective. Soon a dense energy wave, like a zigzag formation, was slowly building in the G-spot area and starting to create a corresponding energy wave in the center of my brain.

My yogic mind got excited. I was now seeing the relationship between the G-spot of stimulation and the center of my brain.

Naomi Wolf, in her book *Vagina*, had spoken about the direct connection between the vagina and the brain. I was experiencing this firsthand in my favorite form of learning, through embodiment. I was now stimulated in every way imaginable.

The vibration spread deep within the whole pelvic region. It was pleasant and calming, yet not arousing or heading me toward any kind of peak or orgasm. The activation was deep. It was deep in the tissues and cells of the whole area. It was deeper than my awareness had ever been in my body.

The tissues of the vaginal walls are special, warm, and thick, sometimes feeling devoid of sensation, and sometimes lighting up in certain circumstances. Each woman has a unique pattern of nerve pathways and therefore a unique experience of sensation. The dense vibration that was moving through my walls was giving me a perception of the internal makeup of my nerve pathways. The sensations continued to amp up in the brain and now also in my throat.

Did you know that the throat tissue and the vaginal tissue are the same? I found that so fascinating when I first learned about it. In my yogic practice, I had begun to experience the connection between body parts when the sensations running down the inside of my legs would relax the outside muscles of my neck. They were directly connected as many of the body parts are.

Now I could feel that the sensations being carefully built at the G-spot were connecting circuitry deep within the tissues of the vagina, throat, and brain.

As this continued, the sensation began to feel less neutral and leaned more toward uncomfortable, and Ben was very sensitive to this. He stopped. Instead of taking me toward G-spot orgasm, he concluded that we should let the energy we had built up circulate in the body and open the pathways more deeply. This would better prepare me for the coming two sessions that would follow over the next four days.

He removed his fingers, covered my body, and had me breathe rapidly for a few moments to oxygenate the cells. Then, after two long deep inhales and exhales, I held my breath and squeezed every muscle of my body as tightly as I could. Then, with a quick release, I collapsed fully onto the table and let the energy, now centered and concentrated in the lower part of my body, flood through every pathway.

Inside my body, the energy ran, forming holographic images of awareness that resembled a scene from a disaster movie. In my pelvis, where energy pathways and channels should have been, were the twisted remains of a freeway interchange with full sections missing. It was as though I were looking at a post-apocalyptic scene.

The energy poured through the region, and wherever a break or twist was present, the energy engulfed it, magically rebuilding it from the matrix up.

Tears flowed down my cheeks as I heard yet another small-child aspect of me began to talk. This little voice of me watched in awe and said, "We were broken but now we're not."

My heart swelled. "Oh my God, we were broken and now we're not!" I felt such compassion for myself. I had lived for many years with this dark and twisted, ignored area of my body. I had cut off my awareness of it in every attempt to be a good girl, constantly fighting the natural urges that begged to be expressed, both sensually and creatively. We were broken and now we weren't. These words were repeated over and over as the little-girl aspect smiled. She was hopeful and was happy to let it all go. Tears just flowed and flowed down my cheeks as the energy comforted me from the inside out. I truly had no idea.

After water and a conversation with Ben and Jen, I went back to my hotel with home-play instructions. We needed to build a mind circuit in the brain that would allow me to experience G-spot manipulation as pleasure. In doing so, I would work with both the G-spot and clitoris at the same time. That way I could connect the pleasure of a clitoris-initiated orgasm to G-spot stimulation. I would need to do this multiple times before I returned on Wednesday.

I felt quiet and a little sad, yet skirting the reality of what I was truly feeling. The whole session felt good and safe, and I felt absolutely comfortable with Ben and Jen. But somewhere in me, I was retreating and scared. I sat with those feelings over room service on my comfy bed and just watched and felt and listened.

All along, I had been afraid of how it would feel to really let go. Would I survive such a thing in my mind? Would it overtake me and make me fully lose control of myself? Would it make me bad?

Now the fear had shifted. What if I couldn't let go? Ben had stopped before attempting to take me to G-spot orgasm that day. Was it because I was broken? Maybe I couldn't really do this at all. Maybe I was defective.

They were diligent in keeping tabs on me the whole time. That evening, I received a call checking in, and, at that moment, I shared what had arose. Ben remarked that he and Jen were surprised that I had not brought it up before, as it is something every woman fears. They did not reassure me nor tell me that I could be correct. They just listened and acknowledged me. That was perfect.

I decided to become an expert. I opened my computer and began searching the Internet for the best diagram of the G-spot and the most precise instructions on approach. My mind wanted to become part of this, and so I let her get all technical.

It took some practice to feel pleasure in stimulating this area, but I achieved this and was also feeling a milder form of the zigzagging energy sensation that Ben had brought me to earlier that day. I was ready to try again. But first, I would have a whole day off to integrate and continue to explore self-play. I was shifting. I was really doing this.

Tuesday morning came, and I trekked over to the neighborhood Starbucks with my laptop. A cozy latte and scone were perfect starts to what would flow through my fingertips, as I recorded the notes of my experience so far. But first, I would check my messages and look after anything the world needed from me.

Into my e-mail I ventured, and there was a note from the local Remax Real Estate office in Grande Prairie, where I had lived many years. The brokerage office had been sold, and an audit of their trust account revealed a thousand-dollar credit in my name. Apparently, it had not been returned to me after a real estate offer had been declined.

It was happening. The manifestation effect of the creative energy now flowing more freely was beginning. First, it was the upgraded cab, now it was a good portion of funds to pay for the sessions. The universe was totally reflecting back what I was sending out, creative abundant energy.

Chapter 4

Wednesday arrived. I journeyed over to the house in another black limo, and this time, the driver and I had an instant best-friend connection. He gave me his card and would become my chauffeur for the remainder of my trip. His name was Zoubair. He was a sparkling soul from another country so grateful to be in the US.

As I entered the house, I felt the same rush of energy that I felt the first moment I walked into the room. We sat with tea while we talked of my exploration and experiences. We revisited the affirmations and crafted ones that were more refined as my experience was unfolding.

Ben and Jen enjoyed the story of the money manifestation and giggled, as this was such a common occurrence once women began the process. Many of their clients were highly successful women looking to exponentially accelerate their experiences of life. Ben and Jen were really enjoying my yogic background and all the feedback I could provide on the energetic pathways.

I undressed and popped up onto the table again. I was even more relaxed this time. I basically knew what to expect, and I felt really comfortable in their care. I just wanted to let go and see what would happen today.

Ben began with body massage, this time oil free, and worked his way to arousing me. Jen continued to move the energy and talk with me about the experiences she was seeing arise in the field around my body. She was very good at this and always bang on in her information and advice.

Jen is very unassuming. Absolute radiance shining through a petite and beautiful form. She is gentle and matter-of-fact with a love that radiates naturally. Jen is very angelic.

Ben is tall and enthusiastic. He knows the power and potential of the knowledge that flows through him, and he is so grateful for his life and the opportunity to serve in such a profound way.

You can call what they do healing and release, but, in truth, it is a goddess awakening. They facilitate the clearing of the goddess' true pathway of expression through her sensuality and pure flowing creativity. They awaken a circuitry of pathways that are built right into the female anatomy, lying dormant under the masks of puritanical programming that our Western culture perpetuates.

Ben has sourced the method to open the circuitry, and I, in my internal body awareness, was seeing and sensing it in a very detailed graphic manner. The body is absolutely the true university.

Ben's enthusiasm gives him that hero-like quality, and let me tell you, Ben Rode is a hero for the goddess, and I am deeply grateful that he and Jen have said yes to what is being asked of them by spirit. Not many people I know would be well suited for this vocation.

The extra beauty of this couple is that they are twin flames. Now I'll be honest and share that I have avoided any exploration of the concept of twin flames, because it has a fairy-tale feel to it that triggers an aversion within me. I never wanted to hope for a fantasy. Having said that—as Ben and Jen lovingly tell the story of their meeting—one can't help but get caught up in its wave.

Recognition of one another was instant. They spent an evening in the company of mutual friends, and then exchanged conversations over the phone and text for the next month. I don't recall if they spent much time together, but one month after meeting, they moved in together and had sex for the first time. They knew. They truly knew, and when you are in their field, you know, too.

Ben's touch and encouragement led back to the G-spot within my body, and, this time, he had me participating by stroking my clitoris and bringing myself to the crest of the wave of orgasm.

My instructions were to keep myself at the 9.5 mark, 10 being full orgasmic release, and to keep riding along the crest of that wave until the G-spot joined in. I found the edge and rode it, sometimes splashing over for a moment but quickly gliding back. This happened for about ten or so times while Ben was matching my intensity on the G-spot.

The deep body tissue sensations were zigzagging again, and my brain core was vibrating back and forth in my head. I could feel a whole energy circuit from the G-spot run up the inside of my spine, deep into the middle of my body, all the way through the throat, and then into the center of my brain. It was one continuous flow of zigzagging energy, deep and intense. I had never felt this until that week.

I began to feel a sensation of needing to pee, and a little voice on the left side of my head said, *"I think we have to pee. We should stop and do that."*

On the other side of my head, another voice said, *"No, they told us it would feel like this, and it's nothing to worry about."*

The left responded, *"Oh, right. We're okay."*

I witnessed these two voices like spectators and commentators judging an event, as they now began to chatter back and forth in my mind. The sensations built and my awareness followed them, building a whole holographic image of the energetic circuitry within my body. It was fascinating. This was a slow-motion multidimensional experience, with multiple points of awareness and knowledge being both downloaded and remembered in my cellular tissues.

This was compounded by peripheral conversations with my mother and others significant in my early years of training. I was at the epicenter of it all, as though an exploded view of my life and programming were being broadcast all around me in a full-awareness moment.

That's when Tomaya's energy came flooding in. What a beautiful surprise! Tomaya was such a gift in my life for a short window of deep learning and experience. I would cherish him forever.

Chapter 5

The summer just prior, I had arrived in Sedona a few days ahead of the Kundalini Teachers Training, where I would once again teach. I arrived just in time to pick up my dear friend Barb from the Flagstaff airport. We always seemed to converge in the same place at the same time exactly when we needed, and I was so excited, because I love her so dearly, and our meetings always bring such warmth to our souls.

I collected Barb at the airport and quickly drove her down to Sedona for lunch at her favorite restaurant, the Szechuan. This restaurant was located in the same complex as my favorite coffee shop and grocery store. We entered and I smiled as Barb ordered her most favorite meal, and we set to sharing all the antics of our lives since we had last aligned in Peru.

Lunch lingered, and, after a good visit, we headed for the vehicle. Still talking as we left the restaurant, my hands gesturing with each word as I animated a story into full form, we walked by an outdoor table.

Sitting at the table writing in his journal was a man whose presence lit my body up like a light bulb. His eyes rose to meet mine, and a rush of energy ignited between us. I smiled, kept talking and walking, as I searched for the remainder of a breath I could no longer find.

Barb looked at me with total confusion, and then punched me square in the shoulder. "Are you fucking blind!" she exclaimed.

I smiled and closed my eyes as I walked and whispered, "I just can't do this right now."

My body continued down the path to my vehicle, and although we drove away, my energy stood in front of that table, gazing into this man's eyes.

I managed to get through the day but soon found myself back at the scene of the crime, hoping for a second chance to speak to him. I was so overwhelmed in the moment when I first felt him that I did what my pattern typically was—I ran away to find my center.

Three days went by, and, despite my frequent runs to "the spot," he was nowhere to be found, so I resigned myself to a missed opportunity and headed for the yoga studio to greet the new students at the opening orientation.

Into the building walked all these beautiful yogis and yoginis. We had a fully balanced training of half men and half women. This was unheard of in most yogic trainings. We were all very excited by this.

One by one, they arrived in their whites with the familiar new faces, both excited and unsure of what was to come. Everyone who came to the center came for healing as well as learning. It drew in such depths of character with pure hearts of transformation.

And then it happened. The door opened and, at first, I felt him. Then I turned, and sure enough, the man from the restaurant walked through the door, dressed in white. He was my student. His name was Tomaya. Oh no!

I just laughed. The universe takes great delight in putting a new challenge in front of me, and here he was walking through the door. Contact with a student was 100 percent off limits. It was a recipe for a disaster if one went there. I had to fully and completely let this go right there and right then, and so I did.

The training began and my practice showed. I was much more confident, and spirit came through me with much more ease, as I had learned to effectively surrender my ego at the door. I loved the opportunity to be in a community in deep, intensive practice, and to share the transmission that comes through as you fully step out of the way and surrender. Facilitating in the thirty-day practice was a huge gift for me. I marveled in my gratitude every moment of each day.

Having Tomaya in the class was an incredible gift. Together with the other three male students, he held a container of the masculine for all of the females that was incredibly powerful. Tomaya is from Switzerland and moved to Canada some years prior to embark on a life of adventure. He was a wild horse embodied in the idyllic male specimen: six feet tall, fit, and gorgeous. He ran and he biked, and he was a vegan with clear bright eyes and perfect skin.

He would sink into the practices with such depth and reverence, yet wandering to the beat of his own drum as he navigated his own unique response to the experience. As with all who venture down these paths of deep self-immersion, we greet our own obstacles face-to-face and meet them in our own way.

When our practices were coming to a close at the end of a kriya, I would open my eyes to find him gazing toward me with a look of love and fascination. He looked at me like I was the most beautiful woman in the world. It was incredible. It was distant and respectful, yet powerful to be seen this way.

All the while, the sexual energy was bubbling in my groin, constantly there, building. The attraction was intense, and it couldn't be allowed out of my body, so I did what I would have instructed any one of the students to do. I breathed it up. I breathed it directly up my spine.

It is common, when you go into deep experiences with others, that the heart chakra, chakra number 4, opens and radiates as it connects with other open hearts. Then what can easily happen is a pathway between the heart and the sacral opens, chakra number 2. My friend Zac calls it highway 42. Then the heart energy ignites the sexual energy, and things can heat up very quickly.

Well, here I was with a superhighway of fresh pavement between my heart and my sacral, and right before me was a beautiful burnt orange Lamborghini sitting with the motor running. I deserved an award for containing that energy.

Breathing the energy up the spine was working well for the first week, and then Tomaya asked if he could meet with me after class on Saturday to discuss his ideas for a yoga center. I eagerly said yes to tea.

My portion of the teaching on Saturday morning ended, and I headed home to freshen up before meeting him that afternoon. I was excited, and I was trying to tell myself I was just being a good teacher.

I got ready and then noticed that as I walked by the mirror I shied away from looking at my own reflection. Deep down, I knew I was playing with fire, but I had to go. I convinced myself it was no different than meeting any other student in the training. It was just for tea anyway.

We sat at the outside tables of the Heart of Sedona coffee shop and talked about our lives and our philosophies of living. They were matching up the same.

Heat grew and our hearts began to warm like fires trying to merge across a barrier. I loved every moment of the conversation and wanted it to go forever, but I knew that I was truly playing with fire in a game I simply could not allow to start. I would not be able to have tea with him during the training again. I knew this and I easily accepted it.

Monday came and practices resumed. Now I needed to add the practice of frogs to my ritual. First thing in the morning, I would arrive at the center to open it and clear the space for the day. Then I would roll my mat out by the door and begin my own ritual of practice as I prepared for the morning sadhana.

Tomaya was always the first to arrive. I would feel him walk in the door behind me, and I would feel my heart ignite with warmth. I would feel my whole body ignite with warmth.

Up onto my toes, I would go in a squatted position with fingertips on the floor, as I would begin a round of fifty-four frogs, inhaling my buttocks up and exhaling it down. I simply had to burn up the quad muscles of my legs to get the sexual energy to flow, so it would not build and pool and drive me wild in my body. I had to keep the energy moving. It was turning into a river threatening to overflow its banks.

The practices continued, and the group was so phenomenal. They came in at such a high level of personal responsibility that the concepts of the kundalini philosophies were met with intelligence and personal integration. They allowed their true essence to weigh out their experience, and then would choose how deeply it would be integrated.

Mira, our beloved food goddess, together with teachers Hari Jap, Zac, Sydney, Jeff, and I were all in bliss this training. This was an incredible assemblage of souls. They were so much fun, and everything was reaching new heights.

All the trainings are divinely arranged but having a configuration of perfect gender balance took us to levels we had not ever reached. For many women it's easy to be vulnerable and share in the presence of other women. But to do so in a container lovingly held by men was incredible, just as the men's experience to be fully witnessed and accepted by women was profound.

Together our group navigated many deep experiences. We grew close very fast. As much as I was there to facilitate a practice and hold the container, they rapidly taught me immeasurable lessons in full reflection of their growing authenticity.

I looked forward to every moment in that room, and especially the moments when Tomaya would arrive in the morning. He is a highly sensitive being, wide open in all the human design centers, except the sacral and emotional centers, which are defined.

Human design is a lens that takes the full birth information of date, time, and place, and uses astrology, the kabbalah, the i-Ching, and the Hindu chakra system to create a body graph with nine centers and connecting channels between them. The way the chart is defined, by set completions and connections of the channels, reflects much about how a person is designed to live their optimal life. It also reveals challenges the personality will have if not honoring their true form.

When I gave Tomaya's birth information to my human design reader, Terry, many weeks later, she laughed and said, "I don't even need to see a picture of this guy. If he had been born centuries ago, he would have had multiple wives and hundreds of children."

When Tomaya would teach a class, my body would respond to the sound of his voice in ways that opened me up like a flower. My hip joints would release, muscles would relax, and openings would come through in profound degrees. I thought this was happening to everyone by sheer reason of his unique frequency, but maybe it was there just for me.

The weeks moved by, and we were nearing the end. By this time, the runs of energy in my body were continuous and feeling quite natural. I was doing an exceptional job of containing the experience, so that no one could feel it leak out into the space, but Tomaya was starting to simply bloom in the feeling of love and attraction.

Both Tomaya and I had such a reverence for intimate connection with another that neither of us was willing to share our bodies and sexual energy for the sake of physical satisfaction only. It had to be a clear and divine energetic match. Given that, I had not been with anyone for almost a year and a half, and Tomaya had learned to circulate his own energy in a three-year celibacy experience. We were both running intense amounts of energy through our pathways. We were both becoming highly yogically trained to recirculate it with continuous movement, rather than letting the energy be sent out toward another.

I watched as students began to take notice of Tomaya's comments about me and the looks that he gave me. In one circle, we were discussing the element of water, and Tomaya began to share how much he loved to watch me dance because I moved so fluidly.

His statement was directed at my teacher, Sraddha, with whom I was sitting directly beside, and all my energy contracted as I felt my face begin to flush. I glanced to the circle where my dear friend and student, Meghan, sat. Her eyes met mine, and, in an instant, she saw the whole thing and laughed out loud. The energy had come out. Shit!

I recovered quickly while part of me knew a conversation was coming between Meghan and I, and I pondered how I would handle that. The training wasn't over yet. I had to keep this contained.

I knew that if I shared the experience with my teachers, they would counsel me wisely, but then the template would have been given form with words, and that would have made the whole containment and circulation of the energy more difficult. I had done an exceptional job of managing this. Oh my God, I had done a fucking awesome job of containing this! I deserved awards, people!

The end of the week was nearing, and we only had two days in the coming week to complete. It was almost done. By now, the energy streaming up my spine had made me aware of new channels within my body and was fully circulating through my third eye, the roof of my mouth, and down a channel in the front of my body, which opened a free flowing circuit known as the microcosmic orbit.

The microcosmic orbit starts near the tailbone, runs all the way up the spine to the bindu point on the crown of the head, then to the third-eye trigger point at center of the eyebrows, then down through the soft pallet of the mouth. Here one places the tip of their tongue against the roof of the mouth to connect the circuit down the tongue, throat, and all along the front body to restart at the tip of the tailbone. It was fascinating and it was bliss. And it ran continuously, and at times so quickly, that the whole circuit buzzed at once while my cervix bounced freely in my body. I was in a continuous state of ecstatic bliss and it was immensely relaxing.

Chapter 6

The final Saturday of the training, I led the group through their first BreathLight experience. Let's take a quick detour to introduce BreathLight, and then I'll get back to the story as quickly as I can.

BreathLight is a powerful shamanic practice that opens the pathways in the body for the true self to fully express. It is a guided experience using three different breath patterns.

Mikael King had introduced me to the process on a journey in Peru in September 2011. Within ten minutes of entering the practice, I knew I would facilitate it and quickly convinced Mikael to cocreate a series of trainings with me early the next year.

In my experience in the Sacred Valley of Peru, the breath ignited an energy within me that made love to me deep in my cells while bringing in divine knowing of my purpose in the world. The following is an excerpt from my diary about that first experience.

"The double helix pattern of two inhales and one exhale created an energy that had taken over my body entirely. I lay fully surrendered on my mat in the Sacred Valley of Peru, as this spirit-filled energy moved my arms and head on its own. My chest soon began to be lifted up and off the floor like an unconscious woman being lifted by angels. It was fun and it was vulnerable and it was so sensual.

"The energy coursed through my pathways, arousing deeper sensations within the core of my body, and the energy played and danced within my vagina, bouncing my cervix like a drum, only to lead directly into the depths of the tissues of my clitoris in what left me without breath at all. I did not need breath. It was completely unnecessary at this point as I lay in pure ecstatic orgasmic bliss. Oh, I was definitely going to facilitate this!

"Mikael gazed at me with his watchful eye, seeing layers and energies being cleared at different levels of perception. He took excellent care of me as he held a space in which the divine made love to me in that very room.

"I was being completely cleared and opened for the goddess energy, the pure divine sexual energy, to just flood through me. This is the stuff of creation, not something to be ashamed of, as much of my puritan upbringing would have my mind convinced. This was the divine bliss flooding through me, and, in those moments, I had no resistance of any kind. It was pure magic. I was breathless.

"The breath practice shifted, moving from the double-helix breath to a mother-wave breath, in which we inhaled once, long and deep, and then exhaled slowly and fully. It was like an ocean wave. This took me deeper.

"The sensations in my body reduced to a consistent simmer and carried themselves into every single square inch of my cells right out to the tips of each strand of my long blonde hair. I was light itself, glowing through a wide-open vessel. Clarity and knowing of what would come flooded in such a grand state that my mind sat in a state of shock in all that we witnessed. I was being told how life would go, and I was as excited as I was in awe of such possibilities.

"The breath wound down, and we all slowly made our way back up to a seated position in varying states of bliss and release. It was profound all the way around the circle. I had very little words to share. All I said is, 'I must facilitate this.'"

And so I did. I learned the technique from Mikael and had taken literally hundreds of people through transformative practices that opened them up to greater depths of true-self embodiment.

I had wanted to BreathLight the yoga group all the way through the training, but Sraddha wanted to preserve the experience of the traditional lineages so as not to confuse the practices. I completely understood her point of view as she held sacred the ancient teachings of yoga.

This day would be the day, and I was so excited to take them through the breath work. After all they had now experienced in a month of kundalini immersion, the BreathLight would be mind-blowing.

All but one of the students arrived, and we placed their mats in a circle with heads facing inward. Perfect bolsters were placed under their heart centers to exaggerate the opening, and we began the practice. Warm-ups led to the double-helix breath, and, within seconds, these highly open and activated kundalini yogis and yoginis were fully buzzing with the energy of bliss in their pathways.

Some were in various states of tetany contraction, an overstimulation of muscles and nerves that causes the body to lock up in some of the muscles. As last bits of energetic blockage were flooding out the hands and feet, they were jamming up on the way out. We toned to send the sound current through the pathways to easily bust the blocks. All were in a deep state of instant bliss.

I went around the room, reading their intake forms and applying pressure points to their bodies as a divine guardian whispered messages of love and forgiveness into their ears through the channel of my voice. It was a most blissful practice to facilitate and be witness of.

When I reached Tomaya, I found him in full communion with the Holy Spirit, wide open, with the universe flooding through his every cell. He was totally surrendered, completely aware, and one with everything.

The experience wound to completion, and each one rolled from their backs to their fronts, looking like they had just had the best sex of their lives. It was an incredible field of energy to be part of.

Tomaya rolled over, sat up, and then opened his shining eyes; he looked right through my whole essence. Nothing would be holding back his energy now, and I could feel that in every part of my being.

"Day and a half, day and a half, day and a half," I repeated in my head. I only had to get through a day and a half more of practicums and graduation. Surely, I could make that. Look at how well I had done so far!

By now, Tomaya was greeting me in the morning with a hug. He was selective in hugging people, because he is so wide open and he tends to take in everything that is coming through them. But he came to my mat every morning now to wrap his arms around me and warm me with his literal glowing heart. He was on fire.

Morning practice would begin, and I would feel his whole energy signature behind me as though he were holding my body up in a seated position. Soon our shavasanas were finding our energetic bodies on the same mat, cuddled up in each other's arms. "Day and a half, day and a half, day and a half." Surely, I could make it.

Meghan cornered me the night I moved into Joan Kidd's with her. The training was almost over, and the condo where I had been staying needed to be vacated, so I moved down to Joan's for the last leg of my time in Sedona.

Meghan leaned into my bedroom doorway one evening and leisurely said, "I know this isn't really very yogic perhaps, but what is going on between you and Tomaya?" I spilled my guts all over the place like a kid who suddenly realized she ate too much candy. The relief was immense.

I beamed with the light of pure excitement, and Meghan helped me with my "day and a half" chant until the end came. And the end finally came.

We made it all the way to the final hug when we handed him his certificate, and he whispered in my ear that I should meet him at the cafe. I could not wait.

The afternoon came, and there we were right back in the same outdoor patio, having coffee and chatting. Only this time, the energy that had been contained in our bodies was mixing across the table, and soon a stovepipe lava-like channel had ignited from the base of my spine to my heart and out of my mouth came the words, "Am I the only one feeling this?" I was surprised by the sound of my own voice.

Tomaya smiled and said, "No, I feel everything you are feeling and more."

My heart swelled and my worries rose. I was his teacher by all technical terms; this is simply something you just don't do. It never works out. So I shared my worry, and he smiled and said, "Angela, I have never allowed myself to look at you as my teacher. I have just waited." The answer was perfect. We made a date to go hiking two days later.

I was heading to Phoenix the next morning with my new buddy, Frank. Frank and I had shared the condo of our dear friends Daniel and Silviya while they were away in Bulgaria. We were instant best friends.

Frank is from Brazil and is one of the kindest gentlest souls on the planet. He is wide open, gifted, and we see so much cocreation potential between us. Frank has the ability to look into your life and see the spark of your dreams, and then identify all the connections and points of travel to see them realized. Frank literally prepared "The Design of Me," and we were on our way to Phoenix to purchase the MacBook Air that I am currently typing this manuscript on. Frank saw that my writing was the center of all that I would teach, and the computer was a tool he insisted I should have. Tomaya and I would hike the morning after I returned.

Phoenix was fun, as I love hanging out with Frank, and soon e-mail messages were coming in from Tomaya on my iPhone. He wrote to invite me to merge with him in a full intimate connection of sacred sexual nature. It was the most direct and pure invitation I had ever received in my life. It was clear, and it carried the most pure energy of grace and respect amongst language that showed the level of courage he had risen to. I couldn't type my response fast enough. This was a huge gesture.

Tomaya's design is such that he rarely initiated anything in his life with women. He would simply consider invitations and choose. And believe me, this man gets invitations. This time he was asking for what he wanted, and this came as a result of how our charts combined. This was a very big deal on all levels.

I wrote and simply said, "Yes." I felt so honored, but I had one thing to do first. I needed to tell my teachers. I would not hide my actions, and I did not want them to find out from anyone else but me. I prepared myself for potential judgment, but I was okay with my own decision in the matter. I just wanted to be honest.

Frank and I arrived back in Sedona later that evening. One more sleep, and I would be with Tomaya. I was so excited.

Seven a.m. arrived, and we met to merge into one vehicle and collect our hiking gear from the yoga center. We tried one trail that was apparently closed due to a bear sighting, and then wandered down onto another trail nearby.

It took him seconds to take my hand in his. It was electric. His hands were so big that mine felt delicate and small. This was a new experience. We walked and felt the warmth build until he could take it no longer.

He stopped, collected me in his arms, and kissed me deeply. I could not breathe, and I did not need to. God, it felt good to be in his arms. This man, no matter what was happening, would gaze at me from across rooms and stare into my eyes like I was the most beautiful woman he had ever seen. It was a feeling I had never experienced, and it begged for me to open further. I was as scared as I was excited. It had been a long time for both of us.

Before I had left Canada for this trip, I found myself lying in bed late at night, feeling that sense of loneliness and aching that comes from the desire to be held and loved. I was okay playing the role of teacher, holding space, and feeling the divine flood through me. It truly filled me to the brim, but I was a woman, too, and I longed to be touched, kissed, and gazed at with such connection.

Most nights, I was okay, but once in a while, I would rise to tears as I would pray to the universe to send me a beautiful connection. I wanted to experience full-blown unconditional love with no attachment and no expectation. I wanted to dive deeply without the complication of relationship. I wanted to simply explore the divine in physical merging. I was so ready, and I longed for it in every cell of my body and every corner of my heart. Here it was.

I was walking the trails and weaving across the creek as the path meandered through the woods of West Fork in the canyon with this Swiss God who gazed at me exactly the way every woman wants to be seen. We held hands, kissed, and felt the heat and urgency to which our bodies wanted to fully experience each other. Tomaya wanted us to be in the perfect setting, and I felt such a relaxed knowing that it would all align as divinely as it had so far and in its perfect timing. There was no pressure, just blissful flow and anticipation.

I saw this man exactly for who he was. A pure wild horse not meant to be fenced or tied down. I didn't want anything from him, except the beauty of the experience, and my free flowing attitude simply heightened the anticipation within him.

Our hike wound to a close, and his lips reached down to taste the saltiness of my shoulder. "Don't shower," he said, "I want to taste all of you."

We drove back into town and parted ways as we prepared for a dinner gathering at Joan's that night. Meghan was treating a bunch of us to a beautiful vegan meal, and amongst the guests would be one more of the yoga students. I would not hide the connection between Tomaya and me, so, as our guests arrived, I simply pulled the other student aside and told him that Tomaya and I were exploring our connection. The student beamed a smile so wide that it warmed us all.

The dinner was amazing, and the company was incredible, but I wanted it to wind to a close, so I could be alone with him. Joan's home is near the Oak Creek at Red Rock Crossing by the Crescent Moon Ranch Park.

The guests left one by one, and Tomaya and I decided to venture down to the creek to sit by the water. I took my alpaca poncho with me, and we ventured out.

A short walk and Tomaya led me through the trees across a small stream to the edge of the big creek. In the distance was Cathedral Rock under the light of the blue full moon in August 2012. The air was electric, and the cicadas were singing in the trees.

The creek rushed by, and the sound of the water relaxed every part of me as I spread my poncho out on the flat red rock and sat down. Tomaya sat behind, supporting me in his arms. It was exactly as I had felt each morning in our sadhana practice, only now his lean and muscular body vibrated behind me. I quickly turned around and wrapped my legs around him, being received in his embrace.

His hands slid around my back, and he kissed me deeply, then pulled me back to look into my eyes with such intent. I reached the bottom corners of my shirt with crossed arms and pulled it up and over my head. The moon shone on my naked breasts, and fire raced through his veins.

Soon we were fully unclothed sitting on that blanket, becoming more and more heightened by the dance of energy between our skin. It had been so long for both of us, and, suddenly, it was worth every moment of the wait. I was so wet. I was so incredibly wet.

As though my body were a delicate vase, his hands picked me up by the waist, and he set me upon him. I slid down, bringing him fully inside with a gasp that made me wonder how deeply he would touch me. I opened fully.

There we were under that magical blue moon, August 2012, Sedona, Arizona, fully mesmerized in a connection orchestrated by the divine. No expectations, no attachments, just pure open energetic merging through clear pathways of free flowing hearts, souls, and bodies.

Seconds later, an eagle flew over us with wings flapping so closely that we felt the breeze across our skin. It was absolutely divine. The entire evening was beyond the realms of magic. We spent hours on that flat red rock dancing with God.

We shared three more days together in the bliss of this dance, deepening our connection and beginning to imagine a life of sharing this kind of creation more continuously. My heart was cracking open in ways I had not yet known, as I surrendered both my body and my heart to this man. My mind was beginning to form attachments.

Tomaya spent two nights at the house with me. One morning, standing in the kitchen, chatting with Meghan, I found myself wiping counters while she and Tomaya conversed over some topic. I heard their words, but I was floating in a sea of bliss and observation of the tenderness and vulnerability my heart was now feeling. I felt so safe. I was beginning to imagine more.

Tomaya leaned up against the counter, and then pulled my back toward him so he could collect me in his arms and hold me. My body relaxed against him, and I felt every curve of his shape gently pressed against mine, wide open and relaxed.

His hands collected mine and held them to my body as he gently rocked me side to side ever so slightly while he continued his chat with Meghan. At one time, using one of his hands to illustrate his point, he simply shifted his grasp to take both of my hands in his one. His hands were so big. I felt so held, so loved, so cherished. I didn't want it to end.

But soon the day arrived, and we both needed to make our way for the border. We were so adult about it, simply swimming in the bliss and gratitude of the experience while savoring every last second together. I knew in my heart that I wanted to be with him again, and I was beginning to entertain a more deliberate arrangement of timing.

But as Tomaya so carefully shared in the first few teas we had, he doesn't hold the feeling of anything once he is out of the field of another. I could not possibly understand what this meant, especially not in that moment, and especially because he was clearly as in love with me as I was with him.

But that is not what I had prayed to the universe for, and it was not what my soul needed me to experience. So instead of a soon-to-be reunited scenario, the drive in different directions pulled the energy apart, and, with it, opened my heart to the deepest levels of vulnerability I had yet known. I wanted to have the feeling of this love in my life forever, and it was slipping away like water through a sieve. I could do nothing but feel it as the miles went by.

By the time I reached Canada, the energy had shifted, so I messaged Terry to put our human designs together so I could understand why I was feeling this intensely. I had asked the universe for pure unconditional love, and now it was giving me the final experience in the gift, the letting go.

My heart was ripped open, and even though I sat in a tub of water filled with longing, the tears flowed without resistance in a way that had such a flavor of bliss. I was wide open, and even though I felt sadness and longing, it was as beautiful as the bliss of the connection was. I was purely raw and real. So much gratitude filled me to have been graced with such an experience and to be left so wide open in my heart. I would never be the same again.

Terry quickly explained that because of his wide-open chart and nature, he could not hold the feeling of me within him. The moment he was out of my field, it would change for him. It didn't mean the connection wasn't real; it just meant that he couldn't contain it like I could. She said, "All you have to do is show up in his coffee shop, and it will be the same, Angela." I couldn't do it.

Tomaya shared that all of his life, he had responded to the requests, and that women always wanted the picket fence with him. He wasn't built for it, and so he would move away from it anytime he felt it, because it always meant that he would hurt them.

In truth he was just a beautiful wide-open vessel. He was a master of honoring impermanence by letting each moment go as it passed through his awareness. He greeted each moment as a gift from God and then surrendered it to welcome the next.

He had chosen me. He asked permission. He sought me out. He needed to know it was real. I could arrive in his coffee shop and continue the experience, but he would never know that he wanted it. It felt manipulative, and I would have no part in that. I gave it back to the universe. If the universe truly wanted us to be together, surely, she would orchestrate it as beautifully as she had done the first time. And I let go.

Our e-mails continue two years away from that beautiful full moon. It has left an impression so deep that few have come into my sphere of recognition. And even as I write these past two days, the e-mails come in from Tomaya. I bet he feels every word I've just written. The universe loves us. I am humbled by the scope of what I have been gifted in this life to experience.

And, as much as Tomaya is a major highlight in my life, he is also a beginning of so much more that comes. I love him to the depths of his soul, and I look forward to the next time the universe dances us into the same space and time, even if that only means tea and a smile. What a gift that I should be so lucky to have received!

And now here he was, in my Explosive Sexual Healing session, energetically smiling at me from the end of the massage table, smiling at me to remind me that I am the most beautiful woman in the world, inviting me to see this for myself.

And he is right. I could finally see myself, right there in that very moment, on that very massage table, giving myself permission to be the most beautiful woman in the world and giving myself full permission to just let go at the very same time.

Chapter 7

I could feel the energy coursing through my body, the heat flushing my cells, and the presence of my whole divine self flooding in, expressing in ecstatic pleasure.

As Ben's fingers activated the G-spot, mine were surfing the wave of the clitoris to the crest of yet another peaking orgasm.

Then everything climaxed in a rush of explosive energy, and the sensation of fluid splashing upon my body was felt. In the distance, I heard Ben's voice yell, "Yes! Good, Angela! You are doing it, girl!"

Affirmations about having it all, best-selling books, bringing in the love of my life, being absolutely authentic, rang from Ben's lips. Inside my head, the two little voices began again.

Left said, *"Are we peeing?"*

Right said, *"No, I think we are doing it."*

Left said excitedly, *"We're doing it!"*

Right said, *"Yes! We are doing it!"*

Like a ping-pong game, little statements flew back and forth, fading into the distance, as my awareness immersed more deeply in the center of the experience.

It felt like a control panel in the cradle of my body had been activated, and liquid light was gushing up and out through every cell. The fluid pouring out of my body was energetically charged with magic, pure creative magic.

All the while, liquid light shot up my spine, activating the deep zigzagging energy in my spinal cord and ringing the bell in the center of my brain. As my pineal gland lit up, the light continued to shower 360 degrees from the core of my brain out of my head, showering into my electromagnetic field that now expanded forever. I had never experienced anything like it in my life. I was a literal fountain of magical Shakti energy for many extended minutes.

My body was saturated in awareness and sensation as my mind grasped to frame and classify it all. That's when the mind contracted, and Ben stopped. Giving me the choice, Ben asked if I would like to continue or move into the Big Draw Breath portion.

I was in awe; tears were gently rolling down my cheeks without resistance as I marveled at the realizations and connections forming in my template. My body was a magical portal of the divine flow, and now I not only knew that, I was that. I was wide open and flowing pure magical energy through a whole lens of profound discovery.

I chose the breath and melted under a warm cover into the sensations of the most amazing and brand-new experience. My mouth gaped open in a continuous expression of awe. No words can capture a "first" like this.

Reflecting afterward left me feeling like an explorer. It was like I was a space traveler stranded on an alien planet, having just found an ancient ship from my homeland. Together with my crew, we excitedly dug into the fuselage to find the control panel. Covered with sand and debris from ages passed, with the skeletal remains of the prior crew slumped over keyboards, we cleared the area.

We coordinated a boosting plan, and, with crossed fingers, we fed surges of power to the start button. Would it fire? Would it hold together? And then like magic, the panel ignited, and the entire ship lit into full magical form as the liquid light flowed through the very walls of her structure. My ship was alive, and I could fly. I was fully embodying my ship, and I was flying!

I wrote a lot that night and found myself in a dreamy state of continuous visualization of my future life. I could see the centers I would create, the books I would write, and a man that was coming in. Yes, I saw a man that was coming into my life. He was beautiful!

He came in during that second session. I actually saw his face for a brief moment in my mind's eye, and, moments later, Jen giggled and said, "He's here."

I could not tell what nationality he was, because he has that look of a different culture, and, as I pondered this question, Jen asked it aloud. We both laughed. He is beautiful and whole unto his own self. He will make a wonderful lover, and perhaps even a trail-mate for me. He is a beautiful, passionate shamanic being committed to his path, listening faithfully to his full connection to God. He knows he is directly connected.

This activation was creating interesting and lasting effects all around me. Suddenly, as I walked through public spaces, I began to be acknowledged by the male population in a very reverent way. Doors were opened, respectful smiles and gestures were exchanged, and a heightened sense of honoring was being poured toward me. I felt even more beautiful and seen as a feminine presence of beauty and grace.

The dreamy state of manifestation and visualization continued throughout the whole day off. I tried to write about the experience, but I would wander off into elaborate and vivid imaginings of immense detail.

I could see myself sitting in a comfy leather chair, one that swivels, aboard a private jet awaiting the arrival of my beautiful man. I could see the elegant cabin hostess walking from the galley with a crystal glass filled with beet and greens juice, gently sweetened with apple. Out of my peripheral vision, I caught the beautiful man popping his head into the airplane like a boy playing hide-and-seek, baiting me to chase him with his beautiful and loving smile. The details kept flowing. Beautiful brown eyes that invited me in. I wrote down every impression and soaked in the feelings they brought to me. His eyes were never ending.

A river of flow had opened in my body, igniting electrical circuits that both cleared and activated new areas of awareness. All along, I feared what it would be like to let go only to experience that "letting go" is not the right way to describe it.

The flow just is. It is everywhere, and it is always flowing. There is no limitation, no excess, nothing really even flowing. It is just an opening and expansion. It is our physical vessel that pumps it through the body. It's as simple as inhaling and exhaling.

We have natural flows of expansion and contraction within the body; the mind governs these with varying degrees and levels of automation. But the flow itself or the energy of what that flow is moving, is not actually doing anything but being pure sparkly magic of creation, waiting to be invited through the channel and aimed out into form.

The experience of flow really comes from the suppression and build-up stage. Once the suppression is released, a momentum results as the gate opens, but only for a millisecond when one fully surrenders. It is when we try to cap, contain, or control it that the pressure builds, and one feels the explosive nature. When the surrender comes, you become the energy itself, and the sensations of its full conscious interaction in the body is literally mind-blowing.

I imagine it is like the launch of a space shuttle. So much thrust is needed to propel the craft upward, but once it breaks the barrier of the force of gravity, it just floats effortlessly through space on a trajectory born of its momentum.

Whatever attitude the body channel has taken determines the creation. By attitude, I mean alignment. An alignment consists of the absolute distillation of all thoughts, emotions, intentions, and postures that take aim at a target of focus.

In every moment, this is ever changing but just slightly, like the slow movement of a steering wheel as one rolls at high speeds down the highway. The vehicle reacts to the road surface, the tire balance and alignment, the speed and trajectory. In the same way, the flow simply responds to the attitude of alignment of what is channeling it. And we are channeling it.

It's not this incredible, explosive, mind-collapsing experience to "let go." It's the easiest thing in the world to do, but the mind fears it more than anything. For once you let go, the mind is surrendered.

On that table, I was fortunate enough to experience a release both unexpected and new. A release that sent sparkling sensation of cool activation through a pathway from the G-spot out through the very channels of the clitoris. A release that followed with the sensation of liquid light pouring throughout my whole body and beyond.

Chapter 8

Friday arrived. This would be the last session. What would I expect this time? Now that I had experienced G-spot orgasm and ejaculation, what would be next?

I arrived early to Ben and Jen's, as I had offered to take Ben through a BreathLight activation before we began my session. Jen was in the early stages of her pregnancy and would wait for another opportunity to explore the modality.

Ben was very interested in the training I had received and how it might compliment his process. As one doing both, I could see clearly that this would be a good marriage of modality. Ben's experience of the BreathLight was deep and activating.

Afterward, we drank tea and talked a long time. We had so much to share, and each of us took in every word like it was a fine meal. In our chat, Ben kept repeating that to receive is the ultimate gift one can give.

I heard the words, but they might as well have been a foreign language for all they really meant to me. I noticed this as I found myself repeating them in my head. "Receiving is the ultimate gift one can give." I urged Ben to explain what he meant.

Ben shared that when I came into their space and fully received the process of what they had to share, it allowed them to be seen and the work to be fully appreciated. And to Ben, this was the ultimate gift. This I understood. When I hold space for another's process, I feel so full to witness the beauty and authenticity that pours through them.

Receiving is the ultimate gift. This would be one affirmation today. I wanted that deeply planted in my mind. I wanted to believe in every cell that fully receiving would open the pipeline for a continuous flow of the divine, so that I may have an unending ability to pour it forth for others. I wanted to leave here this day fully surrendered in the flow.

The other focus of this session would be to bring me into connection with this man who was coming into my visions—the man that I called out for in my heart. Ben and Jen saw this beautiful match for me, and Ben drew him into the room through the guided meditation that followed.

I was instructed to visualize all that I wanted to create, and then add in this beautiful soul to share time and connection with on a deep and intimate level.

I couldn't wait to begin. Once again, I was comfortable on the table, and Ben was even more fully open from the breath work I'd taken him through hours earlier. The three of us connected instantly, and Ben began the guided meditation of me connecting with and meeting this lover.

The images came easily when Ben carried forward from my private jet story and took us to where we were deeply embraced in a sensual exchange. His energy filled the room, this man. I could feel his warm heart against mine.

Jen giggled and kept saying, "Oh, I like him so much! I can't wait to meet him, Angela. Bring him here, and we will teach him how to activate you. He is so beautiful."

Then Ben asked me to imagine myself in an embrace with my man. From the warmth of his arms wrapped around me, I was instructed to float up and out of my body—up into space high above the earth, right into the void itself. And in this space, I was to see a room with a beautiful door. Inside this room were the akashic records of all my lives. Each contract was in a leather-bound portfolio upon numerous shelves.

He asked me to see Archangel Metatron open the door and invite me in, as well as to see Archangel Metatron hand me the leather portfolio that contained this current life's contract.

I saw the angel hold the portfolio in his hands, inviting me to open it. As Ben began to instruct me to open and read the contract, the voice in my head whispered, *"Have it all."*

I opened the portfolio, and, in golden shimmering letters that were lifting off the page to meet me, it read, "Have it all."

Ben asked me to look at who had signed the contract, and I saw my own signature. In that moment, my mind jumped in, certain it must be wrong that I signed this important document. Was I allowed? Surely, I must have needed permission. I laughed inside as, once again, I realized how deeply ingrained my mind felt itself unworthy.

One more time, the voice whispered, *"Have it all."* And, out of my lips, I confidently reported, "I get to have it all." This was the plan.

Ben's hands continued to relax and activate my body as I lay on that table, and then we began the deeper process. Once again, Ben stimulated the G-spot, and I stroked the clitoris. My G-spot had changed. It shifted from feeling ridged and stiff to soft and billowy, like the most perfect pillow inviting surrender.

The waves began to build, but this time my mind was trying to manage the process. Now that it knew what could be expected, my mind was trying to run the show. I contracted.

The contractions brought up fears of failure and imperfection, and that began to loop deeper and deeper into further spiraling contractions of unworthiness and failure.

What was happening? I was reversing everything that I had gained. I was shutting down on every level, and my awareness was getting fully trapped inside the mind in all the cycling thoughts and emotions. I had to stop, and so I said, "Ben, please stop for a moment."

I had a very small and slight circuit of sensation running through my body. I sunk into it to bring myself back into the body and out of the mind. I followed my breath, and I followed the pleasurable sensations in my body. It began to work.

Little aspects started popping up with doubts and deeper illusions of low self-worth. I shared that with Ben. He led me through visualizations where I could integrate or remove them. I lay there, feeling scared, defeated, and ashamed that I just couldn't relax when the chips were down. I felt a complete failure, unworthy of all the grand imaginings I had experienced earlier.

"Who on earth did I think I was to believe I could actually have it all?" My mind thought.

And then my little voice came in, compassionate, loving, and kind. She said, *"It's okay. You don't have to do this. You can choose."* She was right. It was still a choice.

No matter what, it was still a choice. My mind quickly deliberated. I was here, right now, in my last session. Chances were pretty good I wouldn't come back to do this again. I was standing at the brink of this cliff, and my mind was fully cowering at the possibility of jumping over—jumping right over into a world of pure conscious flow and receiving. *"Receiving is the ultimate gift,"* echoed in my mind.

I was going to have it all. I signed the contract. It was my purpose, my plan, and my destiny. I was jumping this cliff, and I was choosing to do it now.

I asked Ben to resume. I put all my focus into the body and the sensations. My mind obediently went silent, and soon the sensations were coming back. The dense current was zigzagging deep in the tissues of the body all the way to the brain, and then came the release. Fluid expressed out of my body as the liquid light spread once again. I relaxed, and it all settled to a flow.

Ben and Jen were cheering me along the way as the energy moved through every cell. Several minutes later, it stopped, and Ben asked, "Do you want to keep going? You have more. What do you want, Angela?"

My mind contracted. Every time I was given the chance to ask for something or receive something, I was faced with an internal rule that said I wasn't worthy. A rule that said I was actually a burden to want to be pleasured or to expect someone to take time to do something for me. I saw it crystal clear, and by saying yes to continuing, I would have to break through this rule. It was hard, and my mind fought me. The words "have it all" rang through my head followed by "receiving is the ultimate gift." I said, "Yes, more, I want to go farther."

We began again. Ben and Jen amped up the intensity of the coaching. My mind was panicking for reasons I now couldn't even place; my thoughts ran so fast. Jen instructed, "Tone! Make a deep guttural sound, Angela. Make it loud!"

I began loudly, and the tone got deeper and louder, and then it turned into a scream, a scream that came right from the point Ben's finger was connecting deep in my body and my body erupted like a volcano. Fluid sprayed everywhere to the sound of cheers and them toning right along with me. Every resistance in my mind let go, my body followed, and, for several continuous minutes, I rode the flow to the sound of my own voice and the sensation of tears now being pushed through my eyes.

Later, when I shared that experience with my sister over the phone, I simply laughed and said, "I did what anyone would do when faced with a scary cliff. I ran full speed at it and screamed all the way down." We laughed a long time about that.

In the release, which was happening on every level, my mind was once again placed in the surrendered state of awe. It felt like every aspect of my mind was coming out of its bunker. Like a crowd after a disaster, each aspect stumbled about in shock and wonder.

The realization was clear to every single aspect. They were not in charge of creating flow. My mind was not really even in charge of managing flow. My mind could not grasp any comprehension of the magnitude of the power of the flow.

The magic of abundance and grace and love and joy is natural in the universe. The mind's aspects weren't responsible for its existence. They weren't even responsible for aiming it toward an outcome. The mind was simply the steering wheel, deluded that it was driving. The light kept flooding through my channel to the center of my brain and cascading in every direction like a fountain of magic and divine awareness.

I had, like all of us had, spent generations in a cryogenic-type freeze mode, operating on an autopilot system to sustain myself as I shot deep into my own creation. Now the time had come to wake up. I was waking in every cell as realization after realization flooded through me. This was no longer a truth I believed—it was a truth I embodied.

I was here to open fully. I was here to have it all. Not because I was special or different or worthy or any of that. It was simply because I was in a sea of it all, and all I had to do was recognize that truth.

The outcome was already charted, already recorded in the words upon that contract I had signed. Have it all. This life was about having it all. And the biggest gift I could offer the world was to receive the flow so freely that I would become the flow itself in an embodied conscious form. To listen to the guidance, to respond to the universe's signposts, and to walk in faith and trust through this path of life was truly my only purpose.

"I'm wide open," I said with a gentle smile and look of reverence across my face.

Ben repeated my words in a loud whisper, as he and Jen smiled through eyes that had fully seen me, "Angela, you are wide open. You get to have it all."

Chapter 9

The next day, Zoubair drove me to the airport in his black town car. I would be his last fare that weekend before visiting his family. As we drove past the private airplane hangars, Zoubair glanced into the rearview mirror and said, "I don't know why, but I feel like the next time I collect you from this airport, I will be picking you up from a private jet. I just keep seeing you in a private jet." We laughed. My whole heart smiled.

Hours earlier, I had sat in the neighborhood Starbucks, sipping a latte and writing in my MacBook. A handsome engineer sat beside me and randomly asked me if I was an author. I said, "Yes, soon to be published." It was the first time I had ever declared it aloud.

Then he said, "This will sound crazy, but I just saw you in my mind on the *Oprah* show." Then he said, "You must have some kind of an amazing aura."

I began to wonder if this was the local pickup line, and when he saw that expression on my face, he giggled and gestured me to look at the ordering lineup behind me near the counter. I turned my head to see a long line of men gazing in my direction.

Then my engineer friend said, "See, no one can take their eyes off of you." The men weren't gazing at me with lust in their eyes; it was reverence and pure heightened presence. It was the energy. It was radiating through me. It was pure magical, graceful, creative, sensual bliss. It was the goddess herself and everyone felt her.

Zoubair pulled up to departures, opened my door, and retrieved my suitcase from the trunk. We hugged. Our kindness toward one another had built a beautiful friendship and the knowing that we would see each other once again someday. That felt really good.

After checking in, I rolled through security and found a quiet spot to sit for lunch while I waited to board my flight. I picked up my water bottle in my left hand to take a drink, and my arm began to shake.

I put the bottle down and examined each part of my shoulder and the muscles to see if anything was out of alignment or strained somewhere. Everything felt normal, so I closed my eyes and sank my awareness into my forearm.

Inside the tissues, crouched in a ball, hiding its head was a tiny aspect of me. I listened with such awareness to hear it mutter, "Oh my God, what is she going to do to us next?"

Aw! I felt such compassion. I had taken my mind over repeated cliffs on a journey to find the truth of my pure self. Here was an aspect of my mind that had been scared to cowering by this last adventure. Who could blame it? This one was more than intense. I smiled and came to the realization that it was time to rest my mind and let all that had happened integrate. It was time to write. Back to Sedona I went.

Chapter 10

The completion of Book One, *Avatar Anatomy*, was my top priority. I had a little more than two weeks left in my four-month book-writing sabbatical in Sedona. I would hunker down and get that first draft e-mailed into editing before I left.

I needed an office, so while waiting to board my flight from Oakland to Phoenix, the little voice suggested that I talk to my dear friend Sung about renting the spare office in his brain training facility. He generously replied to my text with an offer to let me use it free of charge until I departed.

I have the most amazing friends. Seriously, I'm not kidding. I meet and converge with the most beautiful souls you could imagine. And if you know me, you know you are one of them. I get the best teachers in their perfect timings, and I make lasting bonds that come from the heart in unions that are met at a perfect resonant depth. I am so blessed.

Sung's office was perfect. I arranged the hundreds of sticky notes I had made onto the walls under categories for each of the book titles. The *Body Ascension Series* name was downloaded to me over the 2012 Christmas shift, and the titles came through once I realized I had more than one book.

Even though I truly had no idea what the scope of each book would end up to be, the guidance had given me enough to be confident that I had the knowledge.

Excuse me a moment while I giggle at that naiveté. Maybe give me more than a moment. Okay, I'm back.

A perfectly designed ergonomic chair for brain training sessions was the centerpiece of the room. I was so happy to jump into it again. I had experienced such profound shift in that chair three years prior when I first encountered Sung and the Brain State Technology process. As I sat reclined and relaxed my body into the writing mode, I pondered the scope of where I had been as I reviewed all the little post-it notes hanging upon the wall.

I began my life very fearful and contracted. I did everything I could to fit in and be what I perceived would make me accepted and loved. As a result, I really didn't exist within my body. I kind of hovered around it, operating my life in an insulated remote-controlled fashion. This felt safer.

The little voice in my head was constant, guiding me in the littlest things and never failing me in the bigger things. All I had to do was listen.

In early 2003, it began to teach me more intensely through many avenues of experience, but mostly through the books of empowerment I was led to absorb and implement into my world. Concepts were being considered and tested until I had a foundation of my own view of how the world worked.

By 2007, I was selling everything and stepping out on a full trust expedition that had no plan but was simply following the next impulse. Selling everything afforded me a bank account that gave me freedom from work, and the opportunity to make self-realization my new full-time study. I invested everything I had in this.

A Sedona Soul Adventure of intuitive readings, breath work, and completely mind-blowing openings led to the ease in letting everything I owned go, so that I could embark on that journey. And the letting go included leaving a six-figure income and a relationship of twenty-six years that could no longer be. This was a major pivot point in my life.

I travelled to Egypt, France, twice in Peru, Kauai, Mexico, Costa Rica, and the western US and Canada. I studied kundalini yoga and now taught it in classes and teacher trainings. I had practiced breath work and now facilitated it. I did belief repatterning and soul-level clearings using systematic methods that helped my mind release illusions of control.

I had done the Neurofeedback Brain Training, Ayahuasca Journeys, and Vipassana meditation. I had done rounds of White Tantric Meditation, and now I had just completed Explosive Sexual Healing.

The biggest gifts I received were the openings in my body that allowed me to feel my true essence within and through, and the ability to hold a field of pure neutrality for myself and others. It is within this field of pure acceptance that unconditional love and healing reside. This is where we witness all that arises without judgment and simply allow it to pass.

The books were birthing through me. I loved to sit in that chair, legs crossed, with my lap desk upon my knee, typing into my little MacBook. Lattes from the Firecreek Cafe across the street kept me in a flow of yummy activation as the words just poured onto the screen. Once Tom Bird had helped me open the flow of my writing, it just came through effortlessly, and I spent hours upon hours just letting it come.

The beauty of the writing experience was the extent of what I learned as the words assembled into the wisest messages shining through my own life experiences. This relaxed the aspects of my mind. Writing *Avatar Anatomy* was integrating the whole beginning of my life into understandings I had not before reached.

The last page of the book ended with me swinging in a hammock in Costa Rica after ten days of ayahuasca plant medicine journeys. I had known it was time to express the energy now pouring through me, and the message was clear from my little voice. She said, "It's time to wake the goddess."

I didn't know what that meant, but I trusted that the voice would teach me. And, of course, it did.

Chapter 11

From Costa Rica, I returned to Sedona in January 2011 to be invited to teach in my first kundalini teacher's training that April. My teacher, Hari Jap, always said that the real learning begins when you teach. He is right. It's like you get an exponential explosion of the aspects of yourself sitting all around you in practice. What you glean from holding space for them, with unconditional love and acceptance, reflects the deepest of lessons in living color all around you. I am so grateful.

Teaching in Sedona led to a return trip to Peru a few months later in September 2011. I was getting restless in my travels and feeling that it was time to look at settling somewhere to share all the gifts that had come. I didn't know what that would look like or where I would do it, but the little voice told me not to worry, that it would give me guidance at the end of the next journey. Peru was calling me back.

Peru is such a place of heart. The people there are so pure in essence that just landing in the country made me feel open. I would go back and journey on my own for a month, I felt. Then my friend Elijah messaged me about an eleven-day journey he and his two friends, Mikael and Veronica, were assembling during that same time frame. I decided to begin my trip by joining them.

A small group of about twelve of us met in Cusco and began our journeys to the Sacred Valley and Machu Picchu. It was like going home. The familiar landmarks, smells, and warm eyes that met me along the way gave such comfort and relaxation to my heart.

Wood-fired pizzas and lattes warmed my tummy and my soul. I could immerse for a whole month and then figure out what was next.

When in the Sacred Valley, we stayed at a charming retreat center near Urubamba called Hatun Wasi. It is run by a Peruvian couple named Isabel and Ernesto. These are some of the most beautiful people I have ever met in my life. I know that I could arrive at their gate and would be welcomed with open arms and loving hugs. They are so precious.

Our group had two houses and a center to play in. We stayed there en route to Machu Picchu and on the way back as well. No matter where I went with this new group, the group I had travelled with the year prior was still energetically in the field. It was a special time for me. My heart was blown wide open as I walked within a waking dream.

Elijah Ray was the man who invited me to join them. I had met him originally in Kauai in 2010 when we both stayed at our mutual friend Amma Sophia's sanctuary. Elijah is an incredibly talented musician and vocalist whose expressions and energetic transmissions are pure angelic in nature.

Before Kauai, many of my friends had asked me if I had heard his music and experienced his presence, but I never seemed to be in the right place at the right time when he would tour Sedona. Now there in Kauai, we were going to be roommates for a month.

Prior to the night he moved in, he invited Sophia and me to Thanksgiving at NoniLand, where he was staying. NoniLand is a beautiful property owned by David Wolfe, world-renowned rock star of raw super foods and longevity.

We ventured to the north end of the island and came into the space just as Elijah was preparing to play and sing for everyone. He is so beautiful. He looks like one would imagine Jesus would look. He is so pure and filled with light.

He began to play as we all sat on the floor around him. My body could not stay down, and, within moments, I rose to my feet and began to move to the incredible sounds of his guitar and his voice. His voice is angelic, powerful, and authentic.

He uses a loop pedal to record tracks of sound and vocals, so he can cycle them while layering additional creations on top. The result was a full band of light, and my body was one of his instruments. All of our bodies were his instruments as he played the cells within them and wove whole templates of geometrical blessings into pure sound form.

The tones and frequencies activated openings of pure trust and surrender to the tenderest parts of innocent levels of our hearts. Then he infused us with love, a love so deep and pure that it melted all masks of illusion away. It was so beautiful. It was like nothing I'd ever heard or felt. It was grace, trust, and love channeled within the spirals of the sound current. It was absolute peace.

Elijah and I slept in rooms side by side and enjoyed our moments of communion in the kitchen over tea and yummy meals. My journey in Kauai was nearing the end when one morning, I woke hearing the voice of a commanding goddess instruct me to give Elijah a specific gift. It was such clear guidance that as I rose, I prepared the gift and a note to accompany it.

My mind began to question my actions, not wanting to make Elijah feel awkward, so I decided I would leave the gift behind when I flew out two days later. I placed it on the night table in an envelope, dressed, and went to join my friends for morning tea.

I walked into the kitchen to find Elijah and Sophia chatting. Elijah was leaning against the counter, sipping from a mug and asking Sophia to share her wisdom of how she came to trust the universe so implicitly to support her.

Sophia was known for unwavering faith in abundance, and even though the universe would sometimes test her to the wire, she never faltered, and the universe never let her down. Elijah had something occur that would delay him from completing his current album, and, as I heard him describe what he needed, I smiled knowing it was exactly what I had just prepared for him.

I inhaled the magic of the moment and simply pivoted on one foot to retrieve what he needed from my room with the note attached.

As I handed him the envelope and shared my story of the goddess that spoke to me, he collected me in his angel wings and smiled as Sophia said, "Yes, just like that. You just trust, and it all works out." We all giggled.

This was just the beginning of knowing that Elijah and I were meant to support each other and cocreate in many ways. That was the reason the universe had brought me to my brother. Little brother is the affection I instantly felt for him, although he is truly my teacher and my very dear friend.

The journey to Peru that we were on was cocreated by Veronica De Aboitiz of Argentina, Elijah, and Elijah's long-time friend, Mikael King, who also came from Kauai. Veronica is a beautiful angel of magical light, delicate and wise. Mikael is the one who taught me BreathLight.

Mikael is a beautiful Asian man with long dark hair who could easily have been a Buddhist monk or big screen actor. His shamanic nature and unwavering discipline led him on a spirit-guided journey to serve the masses through deeply encoded trainings of multidiscipline. The breath was one avenue.

Mikael is a natural-born catalyst and so tends to trigger things that people are ready to look at. It is profound, and I am so grateful for his gifts. It often left me with compassion for him, as he would routinely become the brunt of projection. Somehow, his skin was just thick enough to take it. This gave him the ability to travel to the depths of hell and back along side you without flinching a muscle. He showed up so perfectly to live his dharma with immense conviction.

My first experience of the breath, as I described a few chapters ago, was in that beautiful sanctuary of Hatun Wasi the evening the group and I returned from Machu Picchu.

The experience left me certain within moments of it beginning that I would facilitate the breath process. When we would return to North America, Mikael and I would cocreate trainings in both Kauai and Canada the following year.

Working with Mikael was a great gift, as he is a master of grounding a workshop into form. Not many light workers have this skill. He is now based out of Bali, sharing the BreathLight Bliss through group activations and facilitator trainings. He continues to teach me many things.

Our eleven-day journey together in Peru was ending, and I was heading to my favorite spot of all. I was going to Lake Titicaca. Everyone else had the same plan, so we decided to just keep traveling together.

My dear friend Barb was already in Peru and on a different journey. I remembered seeing her itinerary and cringing at the thought of the pace they would have her moving at. She and I had planned to meet in Puno beside the lake. Sure enough, when I hit Puno, it took me only a few minutes to figure out she needed rescuing.

I collected her and her belongings and took her home to my hotel where she simply rested and breathed in the comfort of a loving friend's care.

Then, a couple of days later, a few of us journeyed over to Bolivia to the Island of the Sun. So far, in my travels, the Island of the Sun is my favorite place on earth. The water of the lake is filled with magical droplets of highly charged liquid. I swam in it every chance I could.

I swim in all the waters of the world. The Mediterranean Sea in France, cenotes in Mexico, oceans on both sides of Costa Rica, and the sacred caves in Kauai. Pretty much every puddle and waterfall I can find, I am in it. Lake Titicaca is beyond them all.

There is one beach on the far side of the Island of the Sun that is quiet and tranquil. The water is shallow and gradually deepens over hundreds of feet. The wavy arrangement of sand crystals and rocks are visible through clear sparkles of sun-infused water. It's cold and it zings the skin as it magically infuses you with codes. Oh, I am right there as I type. I love this place!

My hostel room was modest and only two dollars per night. I could have spent a month on that island eating quinoa and potato soup with fresh-caught fish for meals.

But, eventually, we headed back to Puno a few days before I was to fly for Canada. My month was almost over, and I was still waiting for the guidance of what was next for me.

I had ingrained the habit of following the next impulse of the little voice implicitly, so I would wait for its message. I was promised clear direction on what I would do and where I would do it when the trip ended. And, as promised, two days before my flight, I woke in the middle of the night with clear guidance that I would return to Grande Prairie, Alberta, Canada, and teach.

I saw the images and heard the direction with clarity. I rose in my bed and wrote numerous details onto paper. I knew it had to be real, because I would never have chosen it.

I thought that my days in Grande Prairie would be reserved only for visits to family now that I had embarked out into the big wide world of adventure. Now the voice was sending me home. It had to be guidance. I honestly wasn't very excited, but I would listen. I trusted the guidance without fail. I ceremoniously said yes with a caveat that it must be made easy for me. A bit of an attitude was brewing.

Before I flew, I had the wonderful opportunity to spend the afternoon with just Elijah. We went down to the lake's edge and chatted, sat, and soaked in the beauty of Peru's energy.

Out of my mouth came the request of getting a vocal lesson from him. I almost slapped my mouth shut with my hand; I was so surprised. The truth was that I was really starting to let my voice out when I chanted and when I spoke.

The sound of my voice was becoming pure when I was alone singing. I really wanted to lose my fear of being heard, as I always knew that communicating was my purpose. Each time I would choke up and hold back, I would interfere with the flow. The power of the sound current could not be surpassed in the process of creating. I yearned for a clarity that would express authentic true self. Elijah was the most epic living example of an unimpeded flow of voice I had ever witnessed.

Elijah's beautiful gentle energy made me feel safe, seen, and accepted for exactly who I was in every moment. The little voice knew this, and so it blurted out the request for me. Elijah smiled knowing how difficult it was for me to ask.

He was so happy to say yes. We made plans for the evening to do a full vocal activation. The timing was perfect for both of us.

He began by getting me to sing in tones with him as we moved my voice in octaves up and down. I had to close my eyes, because I was so afraid to let him hear me. Somehow, going within made me feel more invisible.

He was encouraging and looked at me with sincerity when he told me my voice was beautiful. He did some hands-on movement of energy on my back as I sat in front of him, eyes clenched, singing to his instructions. The energy coming through his hands calmed me and opened up pathways in my body for the sound to flow. It was really cool. I was so scared and so excited at the same moment.

Here I was, sitting in front of the person I thought had the most beautiful voice on earth, and I was actually singing for him. It was incredibly empowering.

The next day, as my flight left the airport near Puno, I reflected with such gratitude. The universe had brought me into the company of wonderful examples of the divine masculine. These were beings of pure heart intent, vibrating at high levels of awareness, that were coming into my sphere as teachers and brothers, and sometimes like sons. I felt so blessed.

The beauty of Elijah and Mikael was that they saw in me what I could not yet see. They saw the divine feminine bursting to bloom. They saw the wisdom of the divine mother ready to hold space in a much bigger way and the gift they gave me was the presence of their faith in my true essence to emerge.

How lucky was I to meet, connect, and learn with these powerful examples of awakened males. They truly held a beautiful, supportive, and loving container for me to open my energy pathways and vibrate the essence of my truest expression through the most powerful avenue of the breath and the voice. I love these brothers!

Chapter 12

My flight arrived in Calgary, and the following morning, while in the shower, I declared to the universe that it needed to find me a healthy income and a beautiful place to live in Grande Prairie. I really had an attitude by now. If the guidance was taking me there, it would have to triple prove that it was needed. I'm sure the universe was laughing at what lesson I was to learn.

Within seconds, I heard the guidance that I should phone my friend Rae-Lynne. She had been my personal trainer many years prior, and she lived and worked out of a beautiful 8,000 square-foot home. Occasionally, she would rent out a room or two to engineers and athletes. Maybe she would have a room for me.

Rae-Lynne is a powerful woman. She is built to exceed every limit one could imagine through sheer determination for excellence. She and I would grow to be close friends over the next while. She is one of the most unique people I have ever had the privilege to know.

I messaged her, and, within short order, she was writing to say she had literally just listed a room online the day before. Okay, an 8,000 square-foot home with garage and private suite was a good start, I admitted.

Next, I drove from Calgary to Edmonton to take my first Spiritual Response Therapy training. My dear friend Susan from Sedona had come up to teach a local health clinic the modality, so that they could assist their patients on a deeper energetic level as well as physical level. Once I had learned Susan would be so close to my hometown, I registered for the class to support her and meet like-minded souls.

Within three hours of being in the class, I sold all the pendants I was carrying in Peru. These were the Quantum Vibrational harmonically charged stones that I wrote about in *Avatar Anatomy*. They are amazing tools, and I encourage everyone to check them out for balancing the energy field and encouraging healthy body voltage.

Okay, that was a good sign of income. I liked the way the universe was responding to my list. Perhaps this wouldn't be so bad after all. I couldn't argue with the flow. When you ride the flow, you can be certain you are exactly where you need to be.

To make the story shorter, my return to Grande Prairie was a humbling experience of discovering where I had truly come from. The community in this area is so amazing and diverse in its demographic. People everywhere were coming to the kundalini classes, deepening in the practices and meeting their neighbors for the first time. The energy was bringing more people together and showing me the incredible souls who had been there all along.

When I had left, I could not see them. I was not vibrating in their frequency. Coming back was a beautiful gift, and their support was so incredible that I just wanted to bring them gifts. I wanted to bring them gifts upon gifts of what I had received from my journey.

In my travels, the universe had brought me in contact with so many amazing teachers and modalities, and now that I would spend part of my time in Grande Prairie, I would share them with my northern family.

And so, as I sat in that brain-training chair in Sedona in February 2013, completing my first book's manuscript, I felt gratitude for all that had transpired and what I would be able to share.

February 28 arrived, and I smiled with the biggest grin ever as I hit "send" on the e-mail that held my first draft of *Avatar Anatomy*. The book felt good, but I still wasn't really holding the whole thread of it in my mind. I knew that then, but I trusted the little voice when it told me to send it off to my coach and the style editor for feedback. It was time, and this was a monumental step for me. It felt like time to celebrate.

My good friend Daniel, whose place I had been staying at in Sedona, was so excited for me that the next morning, he handed me the key to his red Carrera Porsche convertible and said, "This is what best-selling authors drive. Have fun for the day, Angela."

I hesitated a moment, and then remembered that receiving was the biggest gift I could give, and Daniel is such a generous and loving being that this was a gift from his heart that could not be refused. I accepted the key and watched him beam with delight. What a fun car!

A day of play and celebration, and, of course, a lot of driving, wound down with numerous hugs from many dear friends. The next morning, I packed my truck and once again headed for Canada.

I love the journey of travel and love the new beginnings that come once I arrive, but leaving was getting harder and harder to do, no matter where I was when I packed my suitcase. I would be back to teach a few months later, but I really didn't want to leave Sedona.

Angela Ditch

The feeling of home was starting to stir in my cells. I had lived the gypsy life for six years now. I wanted to find home. Where was it in a physical sense? I had learned in my journeying that true home was in my body. I could arrive on the scene of any accommodation, whether it was a house, a hotel room, or a two-dollar-per-night hostel in Bolivia, and I could make it my home in less than ten minutes.

The ritual typically involved clearing the frequencies with sound and palo santo, a wood used as a smudge in ceremony. I would unpack to the depth that was practical and stretch right into the whole space with my essence. It felt so good to be flexible and feel comfortable, no matter where I was.

Now I was starting to want to have routine and familiarity. Not so much in the physical space of where I lived, but in the community in which I lived. I was starting to want to settle down and be part of a family.

It didn't matter how many times I came or went—my two main stops were Grande Prairie, where I had lived most of my life, and Sedona, where my soul naturally flew free. It didn't matter how long I was there or gone; the communities opened their loving arms to me every time. I am truly blessed.

But wouldn't it be nice if the universe felt called to settle me down and bring in someone I could play with on an intimate level? I thought. Here I was with all this training, all these activated pathways, all this knowing of potential, and no one in my picture to play with and love.

I had been blessed with such amazing intimate connections that seemed to deepen in succession, but nothing was continuous. If I stopped moving, perhaps that would come. I really wanted to be touched and explored as much as I wanted to dance in the field of conscious merging energies. I wanted to explore the potentials of what could be awakened and created in such divine-union practice.

But mostly, I wanted to be home. The homing beacon was so strong and home really meant being with someone who loved me to the depths of my soul, someone who couldn't wait to take me in his arms.

I'm so glad that I never really understand the implications of what it is I've asked for. I truly only see the idealistic perspective of what I want: it is the journey to experience the desired outcome that will demand nothing less than the full real deal of true self.

You can't fake surrender. You can't fake authenticity. If something false stands in between you and what you've asked for, the universe is more than happy to take you right to it and force your mind to face the illusion. There is no detour around these things; you simply must go through them or over their cliffs.

Waking the Goddess was next to be birthed after *Avatar Anatomy*. The guidance of what subjects were to be written about was given back in December 2012 during a twelve-day period of fasting and seclusion.

You can think you know what something means, but you don't know until you know. Even now, as I type this sentence, I surrender any notion that I know how this book will end or what will be asked of me in order to fully channel its message.

I'm just humbled, and my mind is praying it can handle the jumps ahead. This book made my mind more nervous than ever. Soon I would understand why.

Chapter 13

I arrived back in Canada in early March 2013 after submitting my manuscript for *Avatar Anatomy* and resumed a series of kundalini yoga immersions and BreathLight offerings. The community once again welcomed me and supported me through their participation and ever-expanding awareness.

The community was connecting in leaps and bounds as individuals who had been there all along began to share the wisdom that was waking in them. Initiated by a core group of amazing local teachers, a ripple effect of knowledge was being disseminated throughout the area. The whole community was waking up.

It was clear to me that I should offer group events, along with my practices, to bring in additional teachers who had made an impact on my journey. I wanted to share every gift I could imagine with my hometown community. The natural first gift would be Elijah.

After my first vocal activation in Puno, I received a second one from Elijah in Kauai in January 2012, when Mikael and I cocreated the first BreathLight training. As the training ended, I suggested to Elijah that we do a second round, and this time we invited friends. The very first group activation was born.

After that, Elijah and I would tease about when and where the next one would take place. When I texted Elijah one afternoon to ask if he would love to come to Canada, he replied with a simple, "I say yes to that, Angela!"

September 2013 arrived, and Elijah brought a ray of light into Grande Prairie that united a force of energy into a whole portal of activation. He and I were both listening to the guidance and showing up where spirit wanted us to be, and spirit wanted us to be in Grande Prairie, Alberta, Canada.

Although my heart was giving a gift to the community, it was me who beamed the brightest. I got to sit in the middle of the energy of knowing the beauty of Elijah and the beauty of the community, and how divine the union of the two would be. It was an exceptional weekend to be me.

I radiated knowing that the gift was received on both sides so open-heartedly. Grande Prairie blew Elijah away with the sheer level of authenticity in every soul he encountered. This community demanded the real deal, and once they felt the safety of his pure heart, they opened like blooming roses to receive the gift of his transmission. It was so beautiful to witness.

Elijah was not the only one to see what was happening in Grande Prairie's energy. Friends of mine from all over the planet were contacting me to ask about the energies they could feel emanating from this part of the world. "What is going on up there, Angela?" they would ask.

Everyone wanted an invitation. It was a magical calling from the land itself. The area was showing up as a vital part of the shift happening on the whole earth. With such a rich resource-based economy, Grande Prairie held the container for two distinct energies that were split.

On one level was a spinning energy of industry with its excessive hours, boom-and-bust cycle, and consumerism mentality, and on the other level was a core community of highly spiritually awake and connected teachers and practitioners. The lines between the levels were blurring as they began to merge.

My body used to hurt each time I would return to the fractured energy. The earth was preparing the perfect assemblage of activity to unify these polarities, and it was calling in all the spiritual teachers to assist in the merge. Beyond the core locals who knew it all along were the global emissaries now feeling its pull. An important portal existed here, all along waiting to be opened in a land termed the Peace Country by its settlers.

Once Elijah departed Grande Prairie, all my energy resumed into the final completion of *Avatar Anatomy*. After e-mailing the book to the style editor in February, it took me months to read it again. The process of writing your first book is indescribable to one who hasn't done it. Having said that, everyone should absolutely do it.

I finally opened the file on my computer and braved my mind's fear of reading it once again. I sat with tea and read the first chapter aloud. I cried. It was good. It was really good.

From then on, the whole publishing process was smoother, receiving only delays from my end as I worked through the reality of letting my voice out into the world in such a raw and vulnerable way.

Writing a book is a process of continuous firsts whose effect would surprise me every time. When the ISBN numbers arrived in my e-mail inbox, the reality that this creation was going to be physical and have an identification number worldwide made me giggle like a six-year-old.

Memories of being a little kid stapling folded paper together to look like a book came flooding back in. I always knew I'd be a writer, and now it was actually becoming real.

When the first draft of the paperback arrived by UPS, I held the box to my heart for over two hours before I could open it. I wanted to savor the moment and just meditate with the potential before I actually saw the finished product.

Opening the box and gazing at the first ever printed copy left me in a similar state to the first time I laid eyes on my son. You know the creation is happening, but when you actually get to see it, it blows your mind. It's a crazy powerful experience to write a book. You should totally do it!

Close friends of mine were so supportive and excited that, in December 2013, when the box of the first saleable copies arrived, they eagerly made me pose with the book for photos. I looked like I was having a bowel movement as I squirmed with discomfort, knowing that people were now going to actually read it. My friends laughed and saved every one of the photos, so we could all giggle together one day down the road.

None of that prepared me for what would happen next. People read the book and wrote me personal notes on how it affected them. They talked of streams of energy pouring through them as they read, and felt so identified with my experiences. They commented on how raw and authentic I was. The feedback was so encouraging and kind. I felt loved and appreciated, but beyond that, something entirely different was happening.

As more and more people read the book and saw me for who I was, a field of compassion and love was creating a whole container into which I could rest.

I was wonderful at holding space for everyone while they went through deep transformation, but I didn't often sit in full vulnerability of being held by others.

The more the love poured out toward me, the deeper my heart opened, and the more vulnerable I became. It was immense. People saw me. I was wide open. What could the universe possibly give me next? I felt so full.

Chapter 14

And now we move into a book interrupted, as the original draft that channeled through my hands took a detour and has been changed from this point forward.

I had written twelve more chapters of the most epic, blissful, tragic and perfect story of the deepest love that has come into my life thus far. It was raw and messy and perfect in every single moment.

Once I completed the first draft of the book, I sent it to the person with whom I shared this experience. When I gave the copy to him my heart was heavy with the implications of how it could affect his life. He read with great presence, soaking in the words from every angle imaginable. He spoke of the book's significance, and his gratitude for being the one in the story, and then he asked me, with all of his heart, not to publish it in its current form.

He did so with a surrendered peace and an acceptance that the choice was ultimately mine. He did so with an unwavering faith, knowing that my intention for the book would reveal an even more profound message in the end.

I love this man at a depth never believed possible and I cannot bring myself to hurt him. While I struggled with the difficultly of how I could possibly alter the content, I knew I would honor his request.

Please don't be disappointed. I am not. What good is a book if it causes hurt? Not everyone is open to be as transparent as I am choosing to be. It is not my place to make that choice for them and ultimately I must respect that. We each choose our own paths and who am I to know which one is best for you? In all my writing I endeavor to speak from my own experience and perspective while honoring the divinity of all souls. I know that he feels this deeply in his heart.

But how would I do it? I paced the floor. I was filled with immense conflicting emotion. How would I share the epic nature of the gifts that this story holds, and the ultimate point of the whole book, through anything less than literal truth?

"Make it a dream," the little voice said. The experience was absolutely multidimensional in every way, so a dream seemed a fair representation of the story. *Yes, I suppose I could make it a dream somehow.* I thought.

The first few attempts to write "fiction" left me angry as the words seemed to lack the essence that only truth can carry. The more I deviated from literal reality, the less it seemed like me. Everything I stand for is about deeper and deeper authenticity. The writing didn't feel natural or authentic. I got angry. I was trying to force it.

The first draft, like all my writings, came flooding in from source, shining through the details of my life. It felt like I was betraying the truth when I decided to do it this way. I could not manipulate the manuscript with my mind. It had to come naturally. It had to be rewritten by the book itself. So I prayed.

Somehow the way would be shown. Somehow the essence would come through. I just trusted. Throughout the entire time that the book was channeled, I kept hearing the words, "Trust the book." And now I would trust the book more than ever.

What finally emerged left me marveling in the understanding of multidimensionality, as timelines and events in my life suddenly wove into the absolute realization that time and space are not real. The remaining sections of this book carry all the love and the pain and the bliss of the truth into the depths of an alternate reality, a reality that revealed itself as soon as I surrendered the book and opened my heart and soul to a new possibility.

In the end, the exercise of the two drafts ultimately reveals its perfection. I have unwavering faith in the divine's hand in this, as in all things in my life. What follows proved my knowing that I am not writing a book, the book is writing my life, and it has been since the moment my soul was born. Let's find out together why this has happened, for I cannot wait to marvel in the perfection as I always do in the end.

Chapter 15

A rush of energy rose through my body like a bubble of bliss being released from deep in the water. It was incredible. There I sat, doing a session for a client, tuning into a stream of consciousness that was aligning her energies and thought forms, when an expansion of joy flooded through me.

This particular rush of energy was not for her. It was for me. Wow! It was pure bliss. I took it in deeply, and then surrendered it to be revisited once our session was complete. Then I carried on with my client.

I love doing the private sessions with people and experiencing the divine essence pour through me with knowing and information for them. I always learn so much and get to enjoy that humbled state of surrender that comes when you simply step out of the way and let love and truth guide everything.

It was a new experience to receive such a gift of this rush of energy in every cell of my body that was just for me. It was most definitely for me, and the energy itself was uniquely different. It was otherworldly and seemed to carry an energy of magical tingles, felt, not only upon the skin, but all the way out into the space around me.

The session ended, and as I flipped my laptop open to answer messages and check my Facebook feed, the energy returned, washing over my whole body, while tuning out the sound from my ears and the sight from my eyes. I was calm, suddenly void of all sensation, and then walked into a dimension so vivid, I was sure it was real.

The first sense to return was the sense of smell as a waft of espresso, dripping perfectly into a latte mug, traveled past my nose. Then sights and sounds came back as I found myself sitting at a table with books all around me. It was a book signing event for *Avatar Anatomy*, in a quaint little coffee shop that felt like a familiar place in France.

I had only ever spent a short time in France back in 2008, and, although the scene didn't look familiar, it felt familiar in every way. It felt like I was home. I sat for a moment listening to the varying international languages that always warmed my heart when I traveled. It was comforting to be surrounded by the sounds and inflections of conversation when you understood none of it. The energetics were so fun to experience and the whole scene relaxed me into it like it was a magical book on a cozy winter night.

The scene was being downloaded like a remembrance. I was in France writing my second book and I was teaching yoga and breath, while doing the occasional journey around the countryside to share my current book. The adventure felt amazing and the vividness of it blurred the lines of reality. It was real in every way. *What kind of daydream am I in?* I thought.

A small line of people stood by the table waiting to purchase their signed edition, when the bells on the door jingled as the next customer entered. Again the rush of magical energy danced in my field and tickled my skin. I looked up and around the counter he came, smiling to greet me as light beamed out his soft brown eyes. I felt my lungs expand to take in the entire essence of the moment. There before me, in pure physical form, right there in that coffee shop, stood my best friend in the whole cosmos. My soul swelled with joy as I recognized him completely in every fiber of my being.

I continued giving my presence to the woman in front of me as my peripheral knowing touched his field in my awareness. He ordered his coffee and sat at the table by the window, as he watched me softly through his gentle gaze. His eyes were speaking volumes of knowing and recognition as he waited for the line to clear, and then he rose to come and speak to me. His smile was mesmerizing.

He held up my book and in the most beautiful French accent said, "I have been hearing your name from friends. Then your book ended up on my favorite table under the big tree in the courtyard. I want you to sign my copy. You have been on my heart for days."

"On his heart" - what did that mean? I smiled as I took the book from his hand. He wore a wedding ring and the little voice in my head whispered that he was married. *Good to know.* I thought and I asked for his name.

"Max", he smiled, as though I should know it, "My name is Max," and into the book I wrote the following inscription.

"Thank you for finding me again, Max," and I smiled as my heart radiated the most peaceful and loving warmth I'd ever known.

The book signing wound down, as joyful smiling beings came to support the foreigner and her new book. It seemed everywhere I traveled in the world the communities opened their hearts to me. I felt so blessed. I always felt so blessed. People are amazing no matter where you go.

Max waited and sipped his coffee as he turned the pages of my book, smiling at me with his energy. I felt so much joy being in that space with him. The whole coffee shop elevated in frequency in our combining fields. It was magical.

Afterward we sat for hours, outside in the courtyard, bare feet dangling in the grass, as we leaned on our elbows, at his favorite table, deeply engaged in conversation.

Three more hours of dinner and chatting led us through conversations of common interests. Art, crystals, energy healing, service to our communities, books we'd read, travel and on and on. How had the universe orchestrated it so perfectly that I could venture to this dimension and have this vivid experience? Was it real? Didn't matter, he breathed. My eternal best friend in the whole cosmos physically breathed and was sitting right in front of me.

We came together on such a high level of soul connection that the love that we instantly shared was beyond the body. It didn't matter that he was married or that it was a dream. To have a soul so kindred, to talk to about all the wondrous discoveries of life, in that unexplainable moment, on a level that needed no words, felt amazing.

I had rediscovered the person I had played with in the cosmic sandbox for literal lifetimes. Visions of what we could create together began to flood through both of our minds. The visions came fast, and they were mutual. I could see us in sacred circles connecting fields of energy and light into grids of activation for whole groups of people. It was detailed and profound.

A whole flood of spiritual activation was initiated and accelerated. Time evaporated in the bliss of our merging realities. I was so excited. I had never had such clarity in everything as I did then. I never had such mutual convergence of knowing.

Suddenly my body shook with a jolt back into my session room in Grande Prairie, as I heard my roommate come into the house and shout, "Hey Ang, I'm home and I brought dinner." It was Rae-Lynne.

I laughed as I brought myself back into the space and realized that I had been somewhere entirely different, for God knows how long, as I drifted into the most elaborate daydream I'd ever known. It was so real. He was so real. I could still smell the fragrance of the coffee, and my mind still lingered in that courtyard.

I went upstairs and we enjoyed beautiful quinoa salad with chicken from Escape Bistro, some of the best food in Grande Prairie. Rae-Lynne looked at me and smiled a grin so wide as she began to examine me.

"You look blissed out. Did you meet someone?" she said excitedly.

I giggled inside as I decided to play along. "Yes! I did, " I declared and I began to tell her all about Max.

"It's Saturday night, Angela! Why are you sitting here when you should be out on a date with this man?" she asked, waiting for me to see the obvious.

"Oh no, no, no, no. It's not like that. He's married. We are just friends," I said.

Rae tipped her head forward and looked down her nose from raised eyebrows and decisively said, "Well, he won't be married for long if you let yourself be as lit up as you are." Bliss was sparkling all around me in the air and dancing from my eyes.

I laughed out loud. I couldn't string her along any longer, so I confessed my fantasy or daydream or whatever one could call it. She laughed and groaned, telling me that I maybe should get out more and actually meet real people. We both laughed.

I wandered upstairs, and ran a warm bath, and climbed into it to rinse off the events of the day. As I slid my body down into the water, the same rush of energy returned, taking my senses, and then popping me back into this dream world again.

My naked body was sliding into the hot pools in Rennes Les Bains in Southern France, a place that I had once visited. Ah Europe, where the naked body is honored as natural. *Why did I not live here?* I thought.

The air was fresh in the early hours of the evening. I had the pools all to myself. This was strange. I was absolutely conscious in this other world with full knowing of my normal reality and all the details of this dream world too. *"Alternate dimension"*, my little voice announced. Ok, alternate dimension. That is what we would call it.

My cell phone, lying upon a towel beside me, buzzed to an incoming text. I marveled at the clarity of sensation, as the water droplets dripped from my hands, while I raised them out of the water to check my phone.

It was Max. He was respectfully sitting at a table directly across the bridge from me and wondered if I had time for a walk.

Of course, I thought. There was no other focus in my mind.

We walked down the road and cut off to the right, up into the woods, down a meandering trail. Max talked extensively about his four kids. They were amazing beings of intuitive gifts. They definitely got some of that from their father.

Max's energy was so connected to the earth. It was like he was a conduit of pure God source energy, and with every step, it just flooded from the heavens through his feet to the ground. Everywhere we walked, people, birds, insects and flowers all seemed to rush to his side, smiling and awaiting his love. He was relaxed and wide open.

We neared a sacred site at the top of the hill. It was a large stone that appeared to be in the shape of a chair. The locals had two names for it. One was the Seat of Isis and the other was the Devil's Armchair, two perspectives of diverse description.

Just before it was a small waterway. A stone passage had been created to direct the water. The locals had brought flowers and crystals and offerings to its mouth, treating it like an altar.

Max instructed me to sit upon the bridge of the water passage, and allow my legs to straddle the flow. It would cleanse the energy lines of the body before taking my seat in the chair. I followed his instructions to the letter, and sat with eyes closed, as a flood of energy poured through my whole body, and felt as though it ran right out, like a river, between my legs. I quivered in the sensation. Suddenly the air was more fragrant and the wind swirled against my skin. My senses were not only cleansed, they were now heightened.

After a few moments, he took my hand, smiled and walked me to the chair. The legend was that three energy lay lines ran into the back of the chair and only one came out of the front. Not having any idea what to expect, I simply sat down and closed my eyes. Within seconds, all of the tension in my body began to drip down through the ends of my surrendered toes and fingers.

I felt cleansed, wide open, fully surrendered and whole. As I opened my eyes, he stood with so much light softly radiating from his gaze. Then he took my hand again, and walked me deeper in the woods to another stone structure, which called all my cells toward it. I climbed upon it and lay across it on my back.

Max then walked back to the first chair and sat down. I wanted to be naked in those woods amongst the magic of the trees and the dimming evening light, but instead I closed my eyes and felt a peace I'd never known, as I drifted off to sleep.

Moments later I woke as I felt the coldness of water all around me. I opened my eyes to the confusion of my bathtub in Grande Prairie. *Oh right. That wasn't real.* I remembered.

The tub was really cold. *How long have I been gone?* I wondered.

I drained some cold water and filled it back up with warm water. Whatever was happening to me was crossing back and forth between worlds. Each was as real as the other. And Max! Wow, Max was so beautiful. I had never felt happier and the tension that the chair took from me was gone, and it was noticeable.

Once I was warm, I rose and towel dried my body. It was time for a good sleep. As soon as my head hit the pillow, the little voice began to speak. *"Stay in your heart Angela. It's very important."*

My breath relaxed and I walked across the dimensions and back into the dream once again.

Max was gently shaking my shoulder to wake me upon the rock. It was darker with moonlight shining between the trees. He smiled so warmly. My eyes met his gaze. A gaze so deep that the pool of inviting warmth of his glistening eyes left me with the sound of the splash, as my naked body passed through their surface, on route to depths unknown. I was fearless, like an innocent child, the sensation of the waters rushing against my skin.

His smile widened and his eyes brightened as he felt me in every cell. He had no barriers for me. He was wide open.

Are there boulders on the bottom? Will I hit them? Will a wave pick me up and toss me back upon the shore, or churn me around in emotions that tempt to drown me? I didn't care. This is what I was born for, to remember that I am divinely connected to this being in every sense of the word. There was no end to the depth of him. There was no doubt in my mind.

"Kiss me," my heart whispered silently, "Deeply, now. I want to be touched to the depths of my soul." Then the sleep engulfed me.

I woke a few hours later to the sound of my 4:40 a.m. alarm clock. Soon my yogis and yoginis would arrive for the kundalini chakra intensive I was teaching. It was time to sing in the shower and brew some tea.

The water cascaded over my body, washing the energetic cobwebs of sleep. I love the shower. I get my best inspirations in there and sing beautifully from my heart.

My awareness was drifting. I was thinking about Max, wondering if he was awake, and what time it would be in France. I felt a little uncomfortable. Had my energy crossed lines? I dove right into his eyes the night before and he was married. Right! He was married! Why did he let me in? Why did he invite me all the way in?

That's when that annoying little aspect of the mind, that likes to spoil the fun, cleared its throat and said, "Hehem, Max is a fantasy!" I burst out laughing. Right! Max was a fantasy.

Somehow the lines were blurring. This alternate dimension, as the little voice called it, was so real and now it was bleeding through into my current reality, confusing me about what was actually happening. I couldn't help it. I felt so connected to Max and so excited of when I might see him next.

The students arrived, one by one, and found their place in the studio in our house. Together, the fourteen of us would gather each morning at 6:00 a.m. to chant mantra, open our spines with movement, and then focus into deeper postures to compress tissues and pool frequencies for clearing them. All this would culminate into a distilled activation that would run through the body when we lay down in fully surrendered corpse pose, known as shavasana.

My sister Lorinne was in the circle and she smiled as she hugged me that morning. "Your eyes are extra sparkly today," she said as she winked at me. Lorinne is someone with amazing eyes. When she smiles they flood with rainbows of color that glow and illuminate the room all around you. I love having her in my classes.

Soon opening chants began and somewhere in the distance I could hear Max's voice chanting along with the group. I smiled. He was here in the room. Suddenly I could feel him in every cell. It was so vivid that I actually opened my eyes to see if I could find him. It felt like he was right there on the mat next to me.

We continued with spinal flexes. I love teaching kundalini yoga. As soon as I tune in, a pillar of light floods up my spine and the divine just takes over. My body becomes a tension free conduit of movement and energy, and I get cleansed as the instructions flow out perfectly directed toward all the souls in the room. I could feel Max so vividly in every cell. The dimensions were now somehow fully fusing.

Max's and my energy fields merged completely and expanded throughout the room, connecting all the beings in the space. It took my breath away. We were one humming field of highly activated and elevated souls. It was profound to be in that space. This was the activation I could feel and see when I first met Max. I knew that our combined presence would create a whole new field of opportunity for everyone, but I could never have imagined that it would span the construct of dimensional space and time. I could never have imagined this level of bliss. I was in awe.

Class ended but no one seemed to want to leave the energy. This would become the trend as this group began to experience an energetic like no other. This was seventh dimensional, divine union, embodied bliss, being grounded right here in three-dimensional space. How profound.

My day continued with private sessions, a lunch date and errands, and soon it was time to just collapse on my back and shut down for a few moments. Truthfully I was hoping to jump the dimensions and have tea with Max. Sure enough, that's exactly what happened.

Max loves tea and he loves to make his own blends. I couldn't wait to see him. I walked across the courtyard and he rose from the table nestled under the biggest tree. He met my gaze as I approached. I was going to tell him about the dimensions and how we spanned them, or did he already know? How conscious was he about what was happening? Suddenly a million questions raced through my mind.

What if he thinks I'm crazy? What if I am crazy? All these otherworldly and technically nutty things were happening, but they were real and true. You can't mistake truth. Truth has a vibration that can't be faked. My whole heart beamed with a love so elevated and cosmic that the sight of him reverberated the feeling of epic. Yes, epic has a feeling of cemented knowing in an expanding field of surrendered grace.

I arrived at the table and he wrapped his arms around me to envelope me in an embrace so beautiful. The energy was bubbling between us and he laughed at the joy that was bursting through him. We sat. He poured me tea and our conversation just flowed. We laughed and gestured and carried on. I kicked off my shoes and folded my legs up on the bench and then began to talk with him about the dimensions.

He stopped and became serious as his eyes softened and deepened in an intensity of absolute certainty. It took me by surprise and I held my breath. Then, as he took my hands in his, his heart flooded through his eyes with a love so deep it broadcast through my very soul and out the expanse of my energy field. He reached every cell in my whole body and then beyond. My now fully lit river of Shakti flowing body. Then as the wave returned to him an even more intense flood of it burst through me again. My mouth was agape as I considered a breath that was totally unnecessary. I was in love with this man, in a never-ending dive of merge, in a dimension that felt more like home than my own.

I had stopped mid sentence as I explained the origin from which I came. He lifted one hand and touched his finger to my lips, to stop me from the next word. "I know Angela. I know who you are, and I know who I am, and I know why we have come together," he said with absolute certainty. His eyes were blink less and never-ending.

My phone rang. It jolted me up from my bed at home. *Oh my God! What the hell just happened?* My mind raced. *Oh my God! He is the man from my private jet!* It continued in a never-ending parade of jaw dropping statements, as flashes of those beautiful brown eyes saturated my heart with warmth.

Like puzzle pieces being flipped in sequence, a whole picture and knowing began to reveal itself. He was the man from my Explosive Sexual Healing session whose eyes invited me in. This was crazy. First off, he was married and secondly, he lives in a different fucking dimension!

Do I need medication? I thought.

My body was still vibrating, fully lit up. Even though my physical body was back in the 3-D, sitting on my bed, my energy still sat in the moment, in front of him at that table, gazing into his welcoming soul. He invited me all the way in. Why would he invite me all the way in?

I turned to look at my vision board upon on my bedroom wall. I had made it only weeks before. The top right corner showed pictures of deeply connected souls in the bliss of pure connected ecstatic love. I turned my head up to the heavens and shook it. "Are you fucking kidding me?" I proclaimed. "Married and in an alternate dimension! You brought this epic connection in, and he's married and in an alternate dimension! Seriously!"

I defiantly walked over to my computer, typed the words "AVAILABLE" and "REAL" in large capital letters, printed them, cut them out, and glued them over the top of that entire section of the board.

"There! Is that better? Did I miss some words?" I was pissed off. How could the universe do this to me? How would I contain this level of energy and stay sane? How could this be happening?

"Practice," whispered the little voice. *"You take the energy into the practice and keep your heart open."* Of course, I knew this. I was trained for it.

"Oh my God, not again," I whispered as I collapsed backwards onto my bed, a smile of awestruck joy spreading across my face, fully flowing zigzags of bliss running up my spine. No matter what, he breathed. He was in a physical form, and he breathed. The man on my private jet was somehow real. The soul I had shared lifetimes with breathed and his energy spanned the dimensions to find me.

Chapter 16

The next morning the yoga class arrived and so did Max's energy. The moment we began to chant Ong Namo Guru Dev Namo -which translates as, *"I bow to the divine teacher within"*- Max's voice was in my head and his energy was in the room.

Max and I now practiced together as one field despite the fact that our bodies were separated in time. We simply plugged into one another naturally without any intent or effort. It just was. And it just continued to escalate.

As each day passed, we got more comfortable in the experience of our connection on the energetic level, but still exchanged no words about it. We didn't need them. Our eyes spoke volumes in a momentary glance as our fields vibrated libraries of knowing. It was going very deep, deeper than I had ever known. And it did not disconnect when the class ended. We remained one field of energy, no matter how far apart our physical structures were. I had never felt so safe or had this much trust for anyone in my whole life. I had never been happier. I had found home.

It was what I had asked for. I wanted to merge with a being capable of a never-ending dive, a merge that would beg me to meet it and shine through all the layers of inauthenticity that could stop me from fully surrendering. We must always be careful what we ask for. Oh my God, I had no idea what I had asked for.

I wondered what his human design was so the next opportunity that arose, I asked him for his birth information and returned to 3-D to get my dear friend Terry to check it out.

Terry Stone responded with surprising quickness. It was a Saturday night, and it was as though she were waiting for the incoming message. Her reply was filled with excitement. This was a very big connection. This had the feeling of coming home, soul mates, and pure family. This was deep community service and activation of creative energies with live streaming wisdom and new paradigms to share. She confirmed everything I already felt and saw.

"Am I playing with gasoline and matches, Terry?" I asked, hoping for her to alleviate my worried mind.

"Angela, you are always playing with gasoline and matches. Why would this be different?" She laughed.

We needed to talk about this, Max and I. This would set the course for things to come and alleviate any worries about the energies escalating in the body. We were connecting at such high frequencies that spanned the dimensions. We were capable of doing great things together on a universal level. I couldn't let it get blurred. This man was married and it didn't matter what dimension he was in. We could not allow that line to be crossed.

We sat across that same table, under that beautiful tree, the next Monday evening, as I passed through the portal and vividly described our human design charts. I detailed our personal charts, as well as the combined one.

I explained that, together, we completed all but one center in the design. This meant we had a very deep connection and a little room to breathe. We had many connecting channels that would make us great in service to the collective and would have a fuel of immense creative energy and insights that would shift and mutate templates in the world around us. It was profound and begged to be expressed through collaboration.

There were two things that needed to be cautioned for both of us. One was that I would experience his emotions very deeply and amplified, so I would have to be ready when the waves came. The second was that he would experience the energy of my sacral center with immense amplification, and that he would have to breathe the energy up into the higher centers to avoid it becoming sexual.

My first attempt to explain this left him looking like a confused puppy with his head tipped to one side. I blushed and was more direct. He quickly apologized for embarrassing me, and then giggled as though he couldn't fathom why I would worry. Then I was truly embarrassed.

Excitement returned, and my heart was once again unrestricted and blissed out. My buddy and I were going to do magical things together in some form. Oh my God, this was the gift of an eternity, and it felt like the opening page of a great mythological novel, as two joyful kids entered the Disneyland of energy work that spanned the realms of space and time. It came with the knowing that we were born for this moment in time. We were exactly on purpose. I was so excited.

I was seeing us holding space together in practices and having the magical connection of our energy completely amped up, shifting the templates within the energetic field around us. I saw us in great work together. We were brought together to activate a whole portal, a literal field of universal truth that bridged the span of dimensions. The information was streaming in along with visions so vivid they were like memories. This had to be why. Never had the guidance been this clear or mutually shared with another.

One morning, I was guiding the yoga class in visualization when I suddenly found myself under the cascading flow of a cool waterfall. The water felt so good against my naked skin that I stopped speaking at the end of a sentence in my instruction. Then I felt his hands slide around my body from the back. Startled, I rushed back into the awareness of the room and heard my little voice of discipline remind me that I was teaching a class.

I had not allowed my mind to go to sexual fantasy and I couldn't jump dimensions while in class. I had to stay grounded. I was clear about that with myself. It was vital that I stay grounded. There would be no fantasy with a married man. And there wasn't. I was simply finding myself landed in these scenes, scenes that felt like memory, scenes that felt like they were happening in that moment.

Staying present in the class energy became more challenging each day as our energy bodies began to wander together into deeper and deeper merging and exploration. We were meeting on another realm entirely beyond the dimensions we each lived. This was not a case of fantasy. It was parallel experiences, and we were both having them. No one was creating it through visualization; we were being brought there.

I rose to a whole new level in my teaching skills. I was able to exist in the free flow of this incredible activating energy that the universe was now flooding through me. My body was coursing with juicy, vibrant, sparkling waters that ran twenty-four hours a day unimpeded. It became the most natural feeling on earth yet amped beyond anything I had ever experienced or imagined. All the while, I held a container for all of us to move within the kundalini practices. From a yogic perspective, it was beyond profound.

My cervix bounced in my body like a trampoline destined to launch me upward. I was so ecstatic in every sensual breath. The touch of my clothing heightened everything in my body. I activated everyone in my presence wherever I went. But mostly, as he broadcast through me, my sacral was activating him, and he was being initiated to run the kundalini energy in a very intense way. He was having one continuous kundalini activation that originated in the density of 3-D while trying to walk through his normal life in an entirely different higher dimension.

I already had the training and the practice to run this energy through my circuits. I had done many practices to prepare and strengthen my body for it for six years. I had experienced the gift of Tomaya, and I had experienced the Explosive Sexual Healing. Max had not had any of this training. I worried, as I visited his realm and began to see mental and emotional strain in his body. He looked at me with such internal conflict as though he had lost the greatest love of his life and still yearned for her in that very moment. He was married. I could not forget this. He looked completely tortured.

We needed to cool this down. Perhaps I needed to stay away from him for a while. That seemed a good answer. My mind was finding its usual reasons to run away and suppress. He saw the torment in my eyes and our hearts grew closer.

Chapter 17

Other characters began to appear in the story and amped up the epic nature of what I was feeling, like my dear friend Barb, who called one night from Sedona.

"Angela, what is going on up there? I'm getting a clear message to tell you to keep your heart open and not run away. This is very important. This person you are spending time with is very important in your life. Don't shut down. It's way bigger than you. Way bigger, Angel!" She said this with no background information but knowing how much I liked to run when things got too intense in my life.

It felt like this. It felt so much bigger than either of us. This both excited me and worried me. What body-mind doesn't want to believe its life has great purpose and meaning? I did not want to get caught up in a fantasy.

The annual local fair of healing practitioners was coming up, and my sister Lorinne and I had a booth in it to share the Spiritual Response Therapy. These are source-guided sessions that serve to clear energy pathways, patterns, programs, and such. I was also leading a chanting circle with a gong meditation in the sanctuary to give people a taste of kundalini practices.

As the group gathered for the chanting circle, Max's energy came into the space. I could feel him in every cell now. This was very distracting, but, as soon as I tuned into the energy of the practice, I was solid, wide open, and a pillar of light poured through me to lead the experience. Everything was amped up as the initial guidance said it would be. I just sat back and witnessed. It was such a divine gift for everyone in the room.

I, as a manifesting generator in the human design, have an expanding and enveloping aura. It extends out to meet everyone and holds a field of neutrality and love. Max is a projector. He connects into the sacral of my energy and projects a higher dimensional paradigm through me.

For him, I was an immense and wide-open light to broadcast through. For me, his extension into every corner of my expanse amped up my sacral to shine even brighter. This created perpetual amplification to which we knew no end, as it cycled endlessly, increasing in intensity. It served as an illuminating projected blueprint of our divine-union and seventh-dimension embodied bliss.

God had literally chosen us to bridge the dimensions and bring a whole new paradigm of energy into grounded three-dimensional form. My mind was completely blown. I had never been so expanded and I'd never been happier in my life.

Chapter 18

A week later, the opportunity to go to Sedona was right before me, and it seemed the perfect sign. I accepted. Somehow I believed that if I left Grande Prairie, I would be away from the portal doorway. The thought of being out of his presence for more than one sleep was unfathomable. To me that was proof enough that it was needed. I was now completely attached. Surely, more time and space would cool things off and get us back into the reality of our literal circumstance.

He was married and this had grown beyond the notion of imagination. It was happening in both realms, and it was real in his body, and real in his eyes, as he dealt with the torment of the circumstance. He deeply loved his wife. I knew this. I felt such compassion for him knowing the depth of his heart as my own.

His body was living out the paradox of our situation as his literal spine served to span the distance between us. Pulled in two directions in his heart, and in the paradigm differences of our dimensions, was literally pulling him in half.

He needed to strengthen his nervous and glandular systems so that he could run the energy our combining fields were creating. First, he needed to cool down.

He was trying to hold both ends at once. He was trying to be strong for us all. He was trying to hold the bridge open on his own. The energy needed to flow, and one always has a choice of where to direct it, just no choice to stop it once it ignites. I can't even imagine the torment he was feeling in his mind and body as he willed himself to contain the force of kundalini itself. He is one powerfully strong being. I still marvel when I reflect on what he contained.

Kundalini is often likened to the energy of an atomic bomb. It activates through the portal in the base of the spine and ultimately serves to elevate the consciousness by activating chakras and corresponding centers of the brain. It is the creative, sexual, passionate energy of Shakti. Its purpose is to elevate the consciousness and feed the garden bed where the seeds of spiritual growth and manifestation take root.

Directing the energy was the key, and all he needed to do was make a conscious choice about that. He could breathe it up his spine and circulate it in his body for self-healing and nurturance, and he could take it home to his wife and make deep passionate love to her, sharing its gifts. Both would work effectively to keep it moving and would elevate his consciousness in its path.

Leaving for Sedona was difficult. The night before I drove out of town, I journeyed through the portal to his courtyard. We ate frozen yogurt across a table as our eyes melted completely into each other. I was worried and he felt it. It was time to talk about this directly.

I wanted to bring in the energy of his wife. First, I really wanted to meet her and had said so many times. She needed to be real. That would help me immensely. Then I would cool down, and so would he.

He loved his wife, and his commitment to her was solid, so this was immensely difficult for him. He was being ripped in two. It wasn't that he and I had a chemistry that was lustful. Our entire energy fields and essences were merging into one field all on their own and spanning dimensions to do it. This was the most epic experience of connection either of us had ever encountered, and we had no physical contact other than hugs at the beginning and end of our visits.

So far, most humans have gone whole lives and never experienced anything close to this in the most intimate of sexual encounters. This was beyond us. It was guided. All we had to do was to know each other existed. That's it. It was happening. It just was. We were a matched resonating seventh-dimensional bliss body activation set, holding the frequency and activation of divine union. For "realsy-real," as my friend Paula would say.

He didn't look for this. I certainly didn't look for this in a married person. It just happened. The universe brought us magically together. I told him that soon I would meet someone amazing, that I could play with, that would redirect my energy, and so he needn't worry about lines confusing. He closed his eyes when I stated this, took in a long, deep breath and whispered, "I wanted it to be me."

The sooner I met his wife, the better it would be for all three of us. Deep down, I could not imagine that she didn't feel me in the field. I have very big energy to begin with, and it was radiating like a bomb blast throughout the entire cosmos.

The most important thing was that we knew we had come together for a reason. Our connection was so profound and universally orchestrated.

Max repeated often, "Angela, don't worry. God doesn't make mistakes. We've been brought together for a reason. Please don't run away."

I marveled at his faith. For me, there was only the risk of my heart. For him, it was his whole life and the lives of those he loved most. I felt safe in his faith, and I reminded myself that he came in married for a reason. I needed to remember that. There was a reason. Surely, I would soon understand it.

The trip to Sedona was magical as always. I wrote a lot of this book and walked back into the world of synchronicity on steroids.

The visions I'd been having were now a regular array of memories. Dreams that I'd had in the past were showing up in the actual happenings around me. All the timelines of my life were colliding into this one common field of knowing. I felt like I was playing the leading female role in an epic mythological fantasy movie. Was I going crazy? It was a possibility I thought I should consider.

My little voice gave me clear instructions about the trip, stating that I was going to retrieve some items and receive some messages. I knew that one of the items I was going to be coming home with was a crystal to anchor the portal here in Grande Prairie. It would receive Max's and my merging inter-dimensional energies, and then broadcast them out to the community as a field of pure balanced union.

I could see the crystal in my mind's eye, as clear as could be. It was a cluster of clear points projecting every which way imaginable. But what didn't make sense was that I didn't have extra resources for buying grand crystals. The voice told me it would be a gift, and to just trust that it would come. And so I did.

It was easy to trust. The universe had brought me Max, and along with that came the activation in my body that emitted the energy of magical manifestation. The river of Shakti poured through my circuits giving me all the power to create in three-dimensional form. All I had to do was to breathe and let it be, and wherever I set my vision, in came the result. The circuitry I had awakened in my Explosive Sexual Healing sessions and yoga practices was in full operating mode. I was lit right up all the time. And I mean, all the time!

If people truly understood the power of the goddess's sexual circuitry, they would honor the practice of lovemaking as a sacred offering to the universe, instead of a practice clouded by the shame that religious indoctrination and puritanical programming had created.

The natural unimpeded flow of sensuality showers the magical energy of infinite potential upon the seedbed of the mind. This is how we create. Everyone should be taught this.

The little voice told me to tell my friends what I was looking for, and soon a whole troupe of them was actively seeking the crystal out for me. It was coming. I could feel it.

The whole time, Max was in my field. The words and sounds of each other echoed in my cells. The energetic field we created, through the portal in Grande Prairie, simply expanded 3,300 kilometers farther. In fact, it was getting stronger. I could feel him in every space I journeyed. He was everywhere in the universe. My friends could feel him too, and they smiled with such warmth to experience our resonance.

I could hear him laugh and smile as I took him all over the lands of Sedona. He was with me the whole trip. He couldn't help it.

So many visions were coming in the mind at random times. Some of them took my breath away. They didn't make sense, and yet they did. All of them felt like memories already happened and now would be relived. A love so pure and natural grew like an ocean stretching across the horizon. There was no end to it. The energy flooding through me became so natural and once again created the reverence all around me. I felt like I was floating on my back in that sea of universal love, without a worry in the world.

Each time I would wonder how difficult it was going to be to resist moving toward him physically, I was filled with the grace of God assuring me that it would all be okay. We would figure it out. I needed to simply relax and trust. The energy was being amped for a reason. He was married for a reason. Soon I would understand why.

One afternoon, I sat in meditation upon a flat red rock plateau near Bell Rock. I closed my eyes, and a whole portal doorway opened from where I was right into the space he was sitting. I could see him with a paintbrush in his hand, as vivid as if I was standing there. He was so happy and so beautiful as he created a masterpiece of art upon a canvas in his studio.

It was a painting of a goddess, sitting in the magical stone chair he had taken me to that first night. The representation of the energy lines running into the back of the chair merged and swirled into the three channels that ran up her spine. The single line flowing out the front of the chair, burst from her third eye, symbolizing the pure unification of her body, her mind and her soul. Before her, in the painting, stood an angel with glistening eyes. All the light from her third eye streamed into his, igniting a glow all around him as he received and returned the flow in a perfect circuit of divine union.

As I sat on that beautiful flat red rock, in Sedona, a group of etheric beings stood all around me. They were tall, and I could feel them in my peripheral scanning. They said very clearly, "Max is married."

I whispered aloud with a feeling of shame, "I know."

Then they said, "To you. To you Angela on an even higher dimension in a much different way. You came back together for a reason. Trust. Keep your heart open and trust."

It felt true. It felt true to the depth of everything I'd ever known. I had been searching for home. Max was home.

A funny aspect in my mind broke the seriousness as she stated, "His wife is lucky you are so liberal." I laughed out loud. It was true. In all the feelings and love that was so natural between us, it had nothing to do with his wife. As I searched my feelings, I knew that I did not want him to lose her. She was so important in his life. He loved her and, somehow, I loved her, too.

My heart broke wide open as this natural feeling of caring and nurturing rose in me for his wife. This was my natural reaction. She felt like my family. This was who I truly was. I was so grateful to know that in the moment of actual impulse, this was who I truly was.

Several very gifted friends were anxious to share their insights about messages coming through them for me. Wanda was the first. She had been seeing a group of beings hanging out around me and in Grande Prairie.

She didn't know who they were to begin with. Then it became clear. These were the beings responsible for the creation of the human race. They were coming back to help us in unifying the polarities. Yes, the time of unifying the polarities was upon us. It was the time of the divine union. And a portal of this activation was forming in Grande Prairie.

Wanda told me that Max and I were holding a portal in Grande Prairie that anchored the two merging dimensions, and that it was important that I stay in the bliss field with my heart open. Again, the words came. "Angela, trust and keep your heart open."

Next was Mary. I was facilitating a private BreathLight activation for her, and, during her experience, the beings came through her with a message to tell me that they were real, and that they would be helping me the whole way.

All of this seemed so fantastic on the one hand, and I found one aspect of my mind taking notes on all the potential nutty things that were happening. The list was getting long. All the while, I knew they were true. Truth just is. There is no mistaking it.

All I had to do was look back and see how perfectly orchestrated all my training and experiences had been to get me to this point. I still had no idea how relevant that realization was. I had no idea what I would be asked to hold and to be in the scheme of all that needed to happen.

When you ask the universe for the deepest of merges, it will bring full surrender of the illusion in order to bring in full unity and raw authenticity. The experience will take you through everything in the way. At this moment, I was in bliss. It didn't stop. I had never been happier.

A few days before my return from Sedona, dear friends Daniel and Silviya came to me with the crystal. They had it all along. It was on their deck, having already been cleansed in the creek and cleared by three full moons. It had been prepared for its mission, and it gave them great joy to gift it to me. I was blown away as I gazed at all the points of clear crystal shimmering with rainbows, as it captured and broadcast the light in every direction. It was the exact crystal I saw in my mind. It would radiate the energy through a powerful field. When I shared its description with Max, he called it Angela.

In my quest to find the crystal, six colorful andaras and one green sugary looking crystal also joined the journey destined for Canada. They, too, would play a role within the portal.

Chapter 19

I returned from Sedona, and, within minutes of entering my house, Max was at the dimensional doorway waiting for me. As I walked across the grass to our table under the tree in that beautiful courtyard, I did not know what would happen when he embraced me in a hug. Our energy had amped so much in the weeks apart that I could feel him growing stronger. The visions that I had experienced flashing through my mind were fresh in my memories. My heart raced as I felt his energy near.

I walked closer and saw his sparkling and excited eyes. Our bodies were lit on fire, and our hearts were wide open. I moved in for a warm embrace, and out of my mouth came these words: "If you kiss me, you won't be able to turn back." I was surprised to hear them. Once again, the divine spoke them for me.

He took them in and imprinted them deeply into his whole essence. The embrace was deep and beyond us both as we felt a complete merge and the knowing that it must be surrendered at the same time. Then we simply sat, talked and sipped tea, while our eyes told the story of love and loss at the same moment. Our physical selves were going to be tested. Bliss would now meet its polarity of pain, and would be unified into the field that had captured us—pure unconditional love.

Being apart for those three weeks was intense. We missed each other like twins separated at birth. Being in each other's field now was a feeling of home beyond anything ever known.

Yes, we were in a sea of vibrating sexual energy, palpable in the body, but bigger than that was a field of love so cosmic and deep that it required nothing, just presence. We were a divine union set. We were twins. And even in the intensity of the activation, there was absolute surrender.

I had heard about twin flames right about the same time I heard about soul mates. I ignored both concepts with an overly exaggerated aversion. Both felt like fairy tale concepts of prince charming and "the one" coming in to sweep you off your feet and live happily ever after. I wasn't interested in creating definitions around them.

Not only did those concepts feel unlikely to me, I feared tying my hopes to a lifetime search for such an illusion. I protected my heart. If there were anything to it, I would simply discover it through the course of experience. But the truth was that I felt unworthy and unlovable at the core of my programming, so I feared I would be that one exception to the gift.

"Twin" was the only word I could come up with to describe my connection to this being. I still resisted looking up what that might mean. I didn't want to know. This man was married. I kept repeating and reminding myself of this truth.

We resolved to focus the energies at the elevated levels from which they originated. There was no way I would tear myself away from being near him, but we had to get the sexual energy directed differently. I had to cool my sacral and somehow navigate the now amplified emotions I was running for both of us.

We did conscious prayer around it and spent time seeing if we could exist in a space together and function.

It went well. As he created masterpieces of artwork in his studio space, I began to take the locals through yoga and breath work. I began to create a whole life in this new dimension, sharing the visions and knowings that came through the energies we were awakening. We were excited to be of greater service in all the realms. This was our true nature, and it was comforting to focus the energy toward it. Somehow we were going to anchor divine union all the way back to 3-D. The guidance was clear on the outcome, but the path was not yet fully lit.

Back in 3-D, souls gathered to be part of the magic. It was pure, incredible, magical energy of bliss and creation. This is what happens when the fountain of Shakti runs continuously. It creates a field for seeding miracles and draws in community. All the projects and playshops I was creating were coming into incredible form as the magic of them aligned souls looking for deeper activations and new collaborations. Friends were arriving from the US to teach and share their experiences and gifts with the northern community.

First Wanda arrived to teach medical intuitive training and then Elijah returned to do another round of vocal empowerment and activation. The whole community was buzzing with the excitement of communing in play and practice.

The farmers market became the local gathering spot, as random convergences of beautiful souls would gather, to eat delicious fish tacos, play with crystals and discuss matters of spiritual importance.

I always get the best teachers in the world. They appear at the right time and in the right configuration to deliver the exact message and inspiration needed. That's when two amazing gentlemen appeared in my life.

Each led a diverse life, yet were very spiritually guided and connected to the teachings of the Bible. Neither labeled themselves religious, but they had been well exposed to religion in their lifetime of training. They each sought the truth of love and purity in a deep commitment to serve their fellow man. I was so inspired by the authenticity of their intentions and that they reinforced them through their daily actions.

An instant connection formed between the three of us, seeing that we had much to share with one another. Regular meetups at the market led to the best of conversations and soon included my confession of zero religious training at all.

My family did not belong to a church or subscribe to a particular religion. They didn't have anything bad to say about religion but they also didn't practice one. When I was about eleven I got curious and asked my mother if I might attend the Sunday service down the street at the Lutheran Church. She agreed and helped me to wake and get outfitted in a Sunday best dress for my adventure.

I wandered down the hill and sat on the hard wooden pew by myself. The discussion was so boring and I felt trapped the moment I realized how serious it all was. But, I was polite, so I sat nicely and smiled and took it all in. Then something magical and amazing happened. People began to circulate these beautiful round golden plates, and onto them the congregation began to deposit money.

My first response, as I now sat upright and forward in my seat, was how brilliant this Jesus guy was. Here he had written this book over two thousand years ago and it was still making money. Book clubs all over the world gathered each week to read the book and pay the church money. My little mind could only think the obvious. Nothing could be more important than writing a really good book that lingers on through time. That was the extent of my teachings.

My two beautiful friends laughed as I shared my story and then they told me how lucky I was to begin my exploration at this time in my life. I agreed.

Many great debates left me questioning the basis of their logic. I knew their hearts but some things didn't mesh for me. Instead of writing off the discussions my little voice prompted me to explore more deeply. There must be a bridge between us, I felt, and in order for me to see it, I would need to read the actual book.

I went to my bookshelf and took the King James Version of the Bible off the shelf. I would just read it, simple as that.

Four pages into Genesis and the book landed in the middle of my bed as I began to pace the floor around it, looking at it like an alien invader. It's true. An activist aspect of my nature, I never knew existed, was suddenly fired up to action as I tried to understand how anyone could possibly find any value in this story.

So far as I had read, this "God" they wrote about was an over emotional dictator who didn't like women. Suddenly world history made perfect sense. But wait, this didn't make sense. These two beautiful souls who had entered my life to teach me were not this way. They had hearts of gold and intentions of pure love. *There must be a code.* I thought. *It's got to be a metaphor written at time when this story would represent it. I'll have to find the code.*

I surrendered my efforts and sought diversion through a Netflix video. I popped onto the website and within seconds I was staring at the virtual cover of a miniseries entitled, *The Bible.* Perfect! The impulses always led me to exactly where I needed to be.

Popcorn and a notepad and into the series I wandered. Within moments, the code unfolded like a map of a most epic journey.

Adam and Eve resided in the Garden of Eden, a place of absolute abundance, carefree freedoms and infinite potential. Enticed by the serpent, Eve chooses to eat from the Tree of the Knowledge of Good and Evil and the whole journey begins.

Here is how I saw it. The Garden is the sixth chakra, the pineal and pituitary area of the brain. A unified place to where all the channels that run up the spine join together. When Eve received the activating force of Kundalini, depicted as the serpent, she immediately began to access each hemisphere of the brain separately. This evolved her perception from wholeness to duality.

The moment his happened, Adam was separate from her, and soon he was now eating the same fruit and having the same experience. Confused by their new perceived differences, each created self-judgment that was projected outward toward the other. Soon fig leaves were gathered to cover their naked bodies, hiding their perceived shortcomings and illusory shame.

Afraid of judgment, Adam hid from God for as long as he could, but when God discovered what had happened, he cast them out of the Garden dressed in animal skins. God was the Alpha and the Omega, the beginning and the end. He was both the source of all creation and the result of its evolution as well. The actions of the split sent an echo out into the field that was now returning to reflect a whole new perspective and experience.

Eve was given blame and sentenced to the perpetual wheel of incarnation as the servant of Adam's seed. Adam forsake her and their journey sent them spiraling down the path of separation, down literal pathways in the spine to the lowest center of the root chakra. Adam traveled down Pingala, the solar masculine channel, and Eve traveled down Ida, the lunar feminine channel. They were the farthest from their connection to pure unified source and running on animal instincts alone.

The root chakra experience is all about survival, base instincts and about feeling safe in the body, and supported by mother earth.

As generations began to evolve with the earth, Noah was naturally ascending in his consciousness. God spoke to him and instructed him to build an ark and gather the animals, two by two, to prepare for a great flood. As the waters came falling to the earth, they descended from the chakra above, the sacral.

Sacral is ruled by water, and as the earth was covered and cleansed, Noah and the duality of the species was elevated to the next realm of experience. When the waters receded, the ark docked at what was once the mountain peaks, and a new level of human development had begun.

Here in the chakra of the sacral, the two channels of ida and pingala begin to cross and spiral as they ascended up the spine in a literal ladder of ascent. The human story now became one of balancing polarity and experiencing the world from the perspective of an individual, in creative intimate connection with other individuals. The exploration of sexual energy took its wide polar swing as it moved from obsession to repression.

Abraham came onto the scene and God spoke to him, instructing him to lead the people to the Promised Land. Taking his family and community, he ventured out until the family split to explore two diverse paths.

Abraham's nephew, and a group that followed, headed for the city of Sodom. There they met with the distortion of the sexual energy and the flesh's cravings for excess. Soon God sent two angels to cleanse the earth of the distortion. After much pleading from Abraham, the angels called in the fires from the sky, which then rained down from the third chakra, at the solar plexus.

The fire element that rules the third chakra cleansed the earth of the distortion and then history took the people into 400 years of repression under the rule of slavery. Repression is the opposite of excess and the other polarity was played out.

Next came Moses, who was born of the slaves and then raised by the elite. His discovery of his origin sent him on a journey of self-discovery, where God spoke to him through a burning bush, and instructed him to free his people. He returned to the city and eventually led his people to the Red Sea, where he then parted the waters of the second chakra and walked across toward the Promised Land, arriving firmly in the third chakra and the realms of society, power, authority and fire.

The rules of society were then given to Moses, by God, in the form of the Ten Commandments. Contained in an Ark, the tablets containing these words were carried throughout war. The powers and authorities of the time acted out in an attempt to convert the masses and make their way to the land that God had promised to Abraham.

Many metaphors follow in this chakra. First we have Samson, who was born through Immaculate Conception to assist in the fall of the oppressors. His strength was unstoppable and even when the hair from his head was cut, and they took his sight – the sense associated with the third chakra - he still managed to crush the ruling authority with his faith.

The people then requested a King be appointed, so a representative of God was soon anointing King Saul. Saul or Sol is another word for sun, or Solar. Saul was soon corrupt with power and down from the heart chakra came the pure and gentle David.

David served his king and then braved the might of Goliath, the giant representation of power and war. David's simple heart-centered approach of courage and calmness triumphed as he killed the giant and won the day.

Saul's corruption accelerated as he began to swim in jealousy and the threat of David's rise in popularity. Despite David's opportunity to take the power through force, he spared the king to no avail. For within short order, Saul killed himself and David became the new King.

Once in power, David fell into a great love that shifted into deep lust and his passion got the better of him. He committed adultery and had the woman's husband sent for death. The lessons of the heart began as David now navigated the human containment of such a great force moving within fears born of attachment.

God took David's first son and then bestowed forgiveness, the deepest kindness and representation of the heart's ability to balance and accept. In yogic terms the symbol for the heart chakra is the Star of David.

Next we had Daniel. Daniel and friends were sent to serve the capturing King. Daniel's commitment to prayer spoke to the power of the word, as the focus now became the fifth chakra at the throat. The power of the word is the sound current that interacts with the vast field of infinite potential to create the experiences and forms within our lives.

Through the power of spoken prayer, Daniel and his friends saved themselves from the fate of fire and the wrath of the lions. King Cyrus, impressed by the power of their God, was persuaded to free Daniel and his people and the next adventure in the ascension process began.

What do you think so far? Interesting, isn't it? The Bible appears, in one perspective, to literally be a map of the fall and rise within the body itself. It is a literal Body Ascension Map, spanning the length of the spinal column, telling the story of the chakra experience.

Next we had Jesus. Jesus was conceived by Immaculate Conception and, in fear of his power, the ruling authority issued an order to have all baby boys killed. This was known as the Massacre of Innocence and serves as a most unpleasant representation of people waking up to the truth of the illusion.

Jesus grew to adulthood and embarked on a 40-day journey into the desert, a journey alone where there was no sustenance to support him. He was left only with body, mind and soul. The serpent arrived, once again, to open his consciousness, signifying the rise of Kundalini.

Kundalini energy is present in all spiritual ascensions and awakenings. Often it is incorrectly confused as the Devil himself, but truly it is just a vehicle for opening the perceptions to higher aspects of awareness. Satan's arrival immediately following is merely the test that always follows awakening.

Jesus met Satan and was invited to walk the path of separation. Satan tempted Jesus to accept powerful gifts of wizardry for use in personal gain. Jesus refused. Next he was tempted to doubt his faith and test it. Jesus refused. Finally he was offered all the riches of material wealth. Jesus refused.

These are the wonderful tests that come when one ascends in consciousness to being self-aware. By this time, the initiate has developed more areas of their brain potential and the new spiritual gifts, gifts the yogis call siddhis, are born. Special gifts like controlling the weather, turning water into wine, parting seas, filling baskets with bread and fish, and healing the sick, are now awakened. The choice to use them for the good of the one or the good the whole is presented and the choice of separation or unity is then made.

Still sitting in a place where the mind can rule, the spiritual ego, an ego more powerful that the body ego, was awakened and harnessed by Jesus as he held steady to a higher resonance of unity and said no to Satan's invitation of separation. Adam and Eve, when in the same situation, made the different choice as the focus of their differences embarked them on a journey of separation instead of unity.

Jesus was a gentle and loving presence. He was fully unified and radiating with all the highest aspects of the gifts of God, completely channeling them to the earth, in a quest to lead the way to unity, and the true Promised Land. He was named the savior and the son of God.

This is the journey that Max and I were on. This is the journey we are all on. You can come at it from the yogic path, from the Christian path, from the Buddhists, the Sufis, the Muslims, and on and on, but we are all on the same path of ascension within our literal bodies and spines. The Bible is a story encoded with the map, sharing all the struggles that will need to be met in order to unify the polarities and ascend beyond the realms of separation.

My report to my two loving friends left them smiling and gesturing with "high-fives" as they thoroughly enjoyed my enthusiastic and diligent study of the scriptures. They encouraged me to stop and marvel in the impact of what I had gleaned, as they deeply appreciated my commitment to move past my obvious prejudgments, in search of truth and a bridge between our worlds of understanding.

In the end, we are all on the same quest. We are all going home. Max appeared in my world, from a dimension much higher, to literally extend the length of his spine so we could unify the polarity and ground it to the earth.

For a long time now, my life has proven itself to be deliberate in every way. Every lesson and every experience simply lit more and more of the pathway of this truth. As I walked I would learn the magnitude of the quest. The lessons would be coming faster.

Chapter 20

Max started experiencing sudden jolts of energy in his body shooting at random intermittent moments that felt like lightning bolts. A literal storm was breaking out in spine as he worked to hold the bridge of worlds open. He needed healing work and physical manipulations to relax the muscles in his body. He began to experience more and more physical pain. I could feel it too. Whatever was happening in one, the other got to experience.

We could each be at home in our own dimension, and, suddenly, I would taste and smell popcorn. He was eating it. I would be sipping tulsi rose tea, and he would taste it and inhale its fragrance. If he was sad, I was sad. If I was excited, he was excited. If I thought of him, his energy would fill me. We had no distinction between us.

It was comforting, mesmerizing, and confusing at the same time. My empathy for his wife grew. She must feel me. What grace she must possess to hold a field of space for all of this to occur. I really wanted to meet her, and I still had not. It was time. And then Max arranged it the next time I came through the portal.

Saturday, lunchtime in the courtyard, I walked into the space coming directly from the portal opening. Max, his wife and eldest daughter sat at a table with a huge feast of French delights. His wife is petite and beautiful. She is an amazing mother.

As I walked to meet them, I was curious as to why I felt no worry or guilt. I was as calm as anyone could be.

My mind was confused. Surely, this should be uncomfortable, it thought.

When I got into her energy field, I simply felt compassion and love. I wanted to wrap my arms around her and just take care of her. This was Max's wife, and she was my family, too. This was my pure and natural reaction. My mind was stunned. I was so blown away at how much I liked me in that moment. I was pure love under everything. My truest natural reaction to all that I met was pure unconditional love. I wanted to take nothing from this man and his family. I just loved them. Seeing them together made my heart beam.

Nothing fit the norms of this existence. Nothing in me was matching the regular rules of my 3-D society. I was so proud of myself.

This man was married, and I should have walked 180 degrees in the opposite direction of that portal, the moment I discovered I was in love with him. But this was so beyond earthly realms that I could not have walked away if I had tried. We had some kind of mission to do together, and it had nothing to do with the configuration of our relationship. It was beyond that, and it was beyond us.

How nice it was for me to sit in this multi dimensional perspective, all the while the woman before me was dealing with the reality of who I was in her husband's life. There is no way she could have missed the truth in the energy. I simply felt compassion as I wondered how I would feel to be her?

I had no understanding of their relationship, and I made a conscious point of never asking or sending my own energy there to explore it. What was happening between them was private and a total family matter. She would not find me in the middle of it. I would not interfere. I wished for them to be really happy.

I had spent many moments alone, confused by how easy it was for me to navigate the truth of my feelings without remorse or guilt. The truth was that I knew I could have made love to that man like it was the deepest spiritual practice, and then had dinner with his family a few hours later. Months earlier that realization would have dropped my jaw with disgust, sounding so coldhearted and wrong, but now it just was.

The pure truth is that love knows no boundaries, and unconditional love needs no form. This was true unconditional love. My heart was so free.

I didn't see the experience between us needing a framework of anything. He had a beautiful family, and I would never have dreamed of asking him to give that up. I felt no claim to him and had no desire to hurt his heart or those who loved him. I just felt love and connection. All the 3-D rules around it just seemed wrong.

This was all a moot point anyway, for we were not going to cross that physical line. This had already been firmly decided by Max. His commitment was clear to both of us. He trusted that God had created it all, and he would not run from the experience. There was a profound reason we were brought together, and we would walk its path.

No matter where my reactions came from, the base was pure unconditional love for everyone involved. What was this connection I was in? My mind was being completely rewired. Every platform of "normal" was being torn down in the face of unconditional love and inter-dimensionality.

That is when she smiled at me, rose from the table, and collected me in her arms. Her heart was warm. Her smile was soft. She was genuine in every way.

As she embraced me she spoke softly in my ear. "Max loves you, so I love you. Welcome to our family Angela." My heart melted. This woman knew and she felt it. She was pure unconditional love and my happiness for Max grew knowing that this was life he had created. This was the woman he had married. Why did we not understand this in 3-D? Why did we create a society of people ownership?

This beautiful amazing woman, in this higher dimension, didn't worry about claiming her husband. She only sought to know that he loved. I wanted to bow at her feet. She completely blew me away.

What grace she possessed to hold this field. I would never be the same as she completely honored the truth and then released the outcome to God. Her faith was unwavering. It was amazing.

Still the torment of the suppressed energy was playing out more deeply in Max's spine. My touch on his vertebrae alleviated his pain instantly, as it gave an avenue for the energy to run. I would work on his back now and then to assist.

I could see what was happening in my mind's eye, and I shared all of this knowledge with him, always knowing that ultimately, this was something he would have to reconcile for himself. This was his healing, and it encompassed every scope of the divine masculine's existence, and our complete journey together. He was being stretched throughout all polarity and all dimensions. Somehow he was being asked to hold the entire bridge between worlds, and the bridge was in his very spine. It was profound.

The energy was bringing up every belief pattern and program around love, sexual energy, relationship, taking care of one's self, and man-made ideas of right and wrong. The task for us was to reconcile all the illusions of 3-D right up to 7-D. The struggle for him was pulling his back apart. For me, it was preparing something unimaginable.

One day, as he lay upon the massage table in his art studio, my hands on his body, a sudden powerful surge of energy built between us that was jaw-dropping and so mesmerizing, and then it let go and began to run up his spine. His whole body tensed as he launched himself off the table with eyes as big as saucers. The energy was full primal creative force, and it was purely sexual, coming from the root of our existence and shooting all the way through the crown. All our senses heightened as our chakras blew into expanded activation and began to lock into one another across the room.

Lifetimes of an eternal existence together began to connect us like a zipper being pulled up from its base. The force of the energy was incredible.

He had to leave immediately. This was not the level of energy you attempt to stop, but he had no choice. He ran for the door. I felt terrible. We couldn't control this energy our field created. It was a divine energy beyond us, and now it was flooding through us in the most primal sexual way. A few more seconds, and we would have renovated that room with our bodies.

The next day, the pain was so intense in his whole body and everything took a 90-degree turn.

Chapter 21

The pain knocked him down hard. He pulled his awareness and energy in to simply breathe in the experience. This was important to immobilize him. A blend of herbs and drugs were administered in a combination that surrendered his body, but came with side effects of deep depression and suicidal thoughts. Max was not the only one who was experiencing the effect. Back in 3-D I felt them in my whole body, and a whole new chapter of our connection began.

Our contact lessened, and our mind's began to speculate about what we had done wrong. Our months of unending expanding perpetual bliss had swung right over to the opposite polarity of intense pain and contraction.

Our minds found reasoning to discount the experiences and speculate darker worries and fears. The concoction was playing havoc with me on the energetic level, as it mowed him right over on the physical level. I could barely venture through the magical doorway and often he was nowhere to be found.

I began to have nightmares and visions of taking my own life and making it look like an accident. This got all my yogic attention piqued, as I knew that I was nowhere near this realm of mind-set.

It began on Mother's Day. I was gathered at a family event visiting when all of the sudden, I felt such deep loneliness and separation from everything. Here I was in a room full of people who loved me, and love was the last thing I could feel. It was overwhelming.

I made an excuse to go and worked my way for the door. I didn't even get it closed when the tears came flooding down my cheeks. *What was wrong?* I wondered with such self-compassion.

I drove home and filled my tub with warm water, Epsom salt, sea salt, and baking soda. My favorite crystals were deposited into the water, and I played a healing and soothing mantra in the background. A good array of frequency tools would surely knock out this feeling.

I immersed my body into the water and let the tears flow unimpeded. That's when the visions started. Like a voice whispering in my ear, I could imagine driving over an embankment while texting and making it look like a distracted driver error.

The vision and the voice were so real that I held my breath as though I was suddenly being attacked from an outside force. Many people subscribe to the idea of darker forces and psychic attacks. I'm not one of them. First, I don't want to entertain fearful ideas, and second, if all energy is from pure source, then darker energies simply need more light. I was light. What would I fear?

I sat and went straight into the zero-point perspective of observing and letting whatever came up be simply witnessed and released. The emotional pain was so intense. It was just warming up.

A few days later, the depression lingered. Moments of tears would erupt. Was I missing him? Was I not able to connect that to the emotions I was feeling? It just felt like incredible separation. Like I could not, for the life of me, feel the sense of being loved by anyone at all.

Friday night arrived, and I decided to do my own breath work. Breath work was super effective at blasting out anything that was having trouble moving through the energy bodies. It would surely clear me of the experience.

I set up my crystals all around me with candles and prepared the space with sound and smudge. I set intentions and surrendered with my heart raised upon pillows to open the energy pathways to the heavens.

Within ten minutes, a wave of darkness so intense poured over and through me, showing me a vision of me picking up my long wand-like Lemurian crystal and shoving it through my heart. I could see the blood pouring across my chest in the vision. The pain of separation was indescribable.

I wailed on the floor. Sobs were so intense and so harsh that every muscle in my body tensed. How could I be feeling so much pain? Where was this coming from? My mind raced to protect me.

Should I call my sister? No, she was not feeling well, and she would worry. Should I call my son? I just needed to feel loved. I needed someone to hold me in his or her arms and help me feel some form of love. It was as though I had been cut right off from all existence. I felt I couldn't worry my son either, so I just breathed and watched it all.

"Was this the dark night of the soul everyone talks about?" I heard one aspect of my mind question. I just breathed and wailed and let out the pain as I tried to find some form of self to grab onto. I begged for God to help me.

Every now and then, like a radio station coming temporarily into tune, I could feel him. Max was knocked right down by the pain, and each time he would wake, the torment in his own mind would begin. He felt me and I felt him, and there was nothing we could do when it was happening. We just had to breathe through it.

When I woke Saturday morning, I knew that there was nothing I could not endure after having made it through that night. I moved into a state of prayer for the alignment of energies, and I broadcast more light through my body. Soon my voice sang like angels were pouring through me. The deep separation had oscillated back to pure connected peace.

All I wanted to do was cross over to Max's realm and kidnap him. He needed more care than his reality would give him. He was having a kundalini energy run that went sideways when he tried to suppress the energy instead of letting it pour through him. He needed care that would cool his whole body, reduce inflammation, and settle the kundalini to a simmer. His nerves needed cooling.

He needed coconut water, nutrient rich milk, and electrolytes with aloe vera juice, as well as traction for his spine and more. I paced the floor, knowing that there was nothing I could personally do for him, except see him healed and pray he could hear my suggestions. I did what I could from the required distance. It was torture, and I prayed that he would come off the drugs, so we could both stop feeling their effects.

My emotions were all over the board. I would cry at the drop of a pin, and I had no idea why. Finally, the little voice in my head instructed me to seek a session with Mary Margrave from Sedona. She could help me.

Chapter 22

Mary is a gifted channel whose Christ conscious connection provides deep and accurate insights for people. She is widely sought after and a beautiful friend of mine. Mary is the one with whom I had done the private BreathLight several weeks prior. She is the vessel where the beings came in to give me the message that they were real and here to help me.

I wanted to talk to these beings. I called her, and we set up a time to do a session. I wanted to hear what the beings would share about what had gone wrong and how I could fix it. I caught her up to speed on what was happening, and she went right into action.

The guides opened up the session and wasted no words.

"Where is Max?" they said. He and I had made a pact to meet in this dimension in our current life to unify the polarity and bring an end to the illusions. I came in fully ready. I jumped up on the platform, grabbed the trapeze bar, and swung out, letting go, with heart and trust wide open. Only he was not there to catch me as planned. He was stuck in another dimension.

"Where is Max?!" they exclaimed.

Then they went in to counsel me. They knew I had popped myself up into the higher dimensions and had nothing but compassion for all of us in this situation. Max was married and totally tormented by this experience of division, all while knowing the eternal nature of our connection. I felt compassion. The guides said that wouldn't do.

I was now going to be crucified, they said. I was going to have to drop down fully into this earthly dimension, feel all the abandonment, and feel the sensation of being dropped midair to fully transmute old paradigms and templates that run in the collective human consciousness at this level. I was being setup to take all the pain of centuries of separation through my body and feel it while I held that zero-point perspective, turning it all back into unity. I was left holding the whole thing.

I was going to serve as a literal black hole of transformation for the collective feminine experience of being blamed, denied, forsaken, and abandoned by the divine masculine. Max's absence was going to be the catalyst.

What? This did not sound good, but it was certainly explaining what I had already gone through, feeling all the separation that I had up to that moment.

Mary encouraged me. "You are trained for this, Angela, and you've done it many times in many lives."

They explained that I had opened the channels in my body wide enough that the universe was going to use this channel to flood light into the 3-D plane to shift the whole paradigm. There were many of us now lined up to unify the illusion through our very bodies all over the planet. This wasn't the fun way.

But Max's position in the upper dimension and our unbreakable connection was serving as the gateway for the energy to pour into me.

Mary was right. I was trained for this. I had spent countless hours in meditations and intense practices of simply witnessing and breathing, and letting whatever arose come through to be released. I could do this. I knew I could.

My mind thought, *Okay, crucifixion, that's what? Three days. I can do this.*

Breathwork would speed it up. I would do breath twice a day until I was done. *Thank God for my training. No problem. I've got this,* I thought.

Monday came and the first breath experience started. Within ten minutes, my body was lit up, and I was suddenly channeled into the body of Anne Boleyn as the blade was about to strike her neck.

Anne Boleyn was one of Henry the VIII's wives. He decided to have her beheaded for a reason that escapes me now. Probably because it is hard to fathom that anyone could have an actual reason to execute a beheading. At some level, a love, touted to be the most powerful in its time, turned into an experience of mistrust and the passion turned to anger.

I have walked the imaginings of my own past lives before and felt energies float through my body in the experience. But in this person's life, I may as well have been right there in the moment of her actual execution. I felt it all.

I felt the absolute defeat of self and soul at the knowing that I was being totally forsaken by the man I loved and all the people around me. Not only did this man sentence me to a brutal death, but also not one soul was prepared to stand up and stop it from happening. The love was gone, and the feeling of separation was immense. I cried with such pain in my heart.

The beheading led to being stabbed and then hung and then crucified. The scenes and emotions rolled through me like a movie reel on slow motion. The breath kept steady between sobs, and the energy moved intensely through my cells. It was so real. It was as if I were right there.

And I was doing it. I was diffusing all the pent up energies through my conscious awareness and ability to hold a centered perspective in it all. All the while, the emotions were the most intense I could ever recall.

The session ended and I slept. That was the first one. The next one was gentler, with mostly a pouring of sensation throughout my cells. I cried and the tears now just flowed without the gut-wrenching pain of the earlier experience. I breathed twice a day for six days and moved centuries of pain through my very body.

Not much else was getting accomplished in my life, and this was affecting my income greatly. Old debt leftover from my prior relationship was now becoming a big problem, as I no longer had a stockpile of resources to keep the payments up. My ex-partner had abandoned his part in the repayment, and the pressure of the debt had now immobilized me from my physical movement around the planet.

The stress of this was mounting, and the overwhelming emotions were more than I could take to cope with it all. I just breathed in every moment and put all my circumstances to the side. It was the best I could do.

Max had lost his connection to my world energetically. It hurt immensely to exist at such a level of disconnection after the truth of who we were was so clear. It simply added to the pain I was already in on such a deep soul level. What had gone wrong? Why was this happening? How did I create this?

I wanted to run away. I wanted to get in my truck and drive out of the universe. Oh my God, I wanted to run! This was not an option and it would not have helped anyway.

The guides warned me that if I tried to run away from this or avoid it, it would escalate and become worse. It wasn't a big deal if I just processed the emotion and served as the one to be crucified.

What was a crucifixion anyway? We all think of Jesus hanging upon the cross with arms and feet nailed to the boards. But what was he really doing? He was enduring massive pain in an experience of being totally forsaken by man. Every illusion of fear, every deviation from pure love came up to be balanced and felt through him. Denied and betrayed by his own disciples, he literally processed our sins, and by sins, I mean our illusions. This is what I was being asked to do, and within this, the series of emotions to be transmuted simply shifted from one to the other in a continuous flow of pain.

First, I moved separation, then abandonment, being left holding the bag, being denied, resentment, jealousy, shame, unworthiness, unlovableness, and on and on the emotions came and moved through me. Some that had seemed foreign to me in my own life were being lived through my cells. This was the most intense time in my entire life for pain. I had never experienced emotion of this level ever.

The tears were so regular that I began to worry that I needed help from an outside source. In the worst of the moments, my sister Lorinne and my dear friend Tanis kept such a good eye on me and supported me in every way they could. I would confess my fear of mental instability, and they would laugh and say, "Angela, you are the most sane person I know. None of this feels or sounds off truth." That was immensely comforting.

The one person I would have loved to have leaned on couldn't be there for me. This would be a solo path for each of us for now. I didn't understand why the universe and I had created such a painful time. I kept a faith that it would pass as all things do, and that I would cherish the feeling of hope and optimism that I had totally taken for granted as my normal way of being.

I now knew what it was like to be in depression and not have any idea how to get out of it. You feel literally helpless and in a continuous state of defeat.

The bridge we were navigating felt abandoned. I no longer felt any amount of trust in what would happen next. Max's energy was disappearing altogether; I could no longer feel him in the space around me. That hurt so badly.

I had to get my life back onto a solid track of forward movement. None of the timelines I could see for potentials had happy endings. They were all filled with pain, and no other options were appearing. The guides I spoke to told me that I could collapse them all if I could transmute this collective pain through my body. It was the only option.

But I needed a report card. How was I doing? I needed encouragement. Mary was ready and waiting with open arms, refusing to take money as she felt guided to support me through this process. We were set to talk the next Sunday afternoon.

Chapter 23

Within moments of getting on the phone, Mary was mowed over by the intensity of the energy I was processing. Her body literally curled up in a ball, and she began to weep as she connected to the full scope of what I had been clearing. This had only happened to her one time in the prior ten years. Her guides told her that her body was not strong enough in that moment to hold the immensity of the energy.

We turned the table, and I began to work on her field. It was fascinating. A whole new experience of healing was flooding through my perceptions.

I typically went into a field and connected to the spark of light from which it emanated, but Mary's didn't present itself like this. Her field was like a spinning black hole with galactic arms rotating and spiraling in unison.

I called for a pulse of pure source truth and love to enter her field. Her field had been overwhelmed with emotional toxicity. Her field was trying to process the intensity of centuries of violence toward women. The pain of all the abandonment I was moving was toxic to her energetic presence.

The pulse of pure truth and love began to assist in balancing it. Then I imagined laying her upon a blanket of blue sparkly white light and letting her float out into the void itself.

All around her, I called in the highest of angels and beings to support her as she surrendered all efforts, so she could receive pure source healing. Her spin stopped completely, and her cells expanded apart to create bigger openings between the elements that made her up. All toxicity fell through the open spaces like sand through a screen.

Then fine bottles of essential oils appeared. Two drops of love, three drops of acceptance, one drop of forgiveness, and so on, were deposited in the center of her resting vortex. Then it began to spin again, slowly, building speed.

As all this was happening, Mary began to feel so much better instantly. All this energy I was processing was intensifying in a field of unification that now extended itself into the service of others. It wasn't that I was doing anything other than following the visions that arose and holding a field of pure potential. It was so amazing.

It was a whole new level of effective transformation. The guides had told me that I would act as the black hole itself, the divine feminine void of creation, taking in the polarities and recycling them into new infinite potential creations. It felt so natural. If felt so familiar.

We ended our call, agreeing to let Mary rest for two days, and then try again to see if her body was ready. As I sat on my bed, the first thing that popped into my mind was, *Who's next?* This expanse of energy in my field begged to be put into service.

I instantly thought of Max and prayed to the universe to let me connect to him and work on his body. My heart exploded wide open and the portal opened instantly. I began again, looking for the spark of light, only to find a glowing tube of orangey yellow light surrounding and engulfing his spine and brain as he lay resting on his bed.

It was like a cast of vibrating light that held a specific field of healing energy all around his core column. Once again, my mind was in awe.

I laid him down upon the blanket of sparkly blue white light and floated him into the void. Again, beings of great enlightenment surrounded him closely to his body, while an angel held his hand upon the occipital region, serving as guardian and gatekeeper of the fourth eye, also known as the Mouth of God.

Max rose up and out of his body and merged with my field. We vibrated the same, so it was easy for him to relax in the care of his twin. The beings all around then appeared to take on somber roles as pallbearers while they walked with his body, deeper and deeper into the void.

I wondered what would happen next, and then the beings looked to me and waited. Once again, I saw the molecules that made up Max's body begin to expand in all directions, like an exploded view picture in a parts manual. The space that made up 99.9999 percent of his body was merged with the unified field, and all toxicity simply fell out of his structure, while pulses of love, truth, compassion, and healing set his body to perfect tune.

We remerged his soul and physical body, and then the earth element called to resonate with the bones in his spine. I watched as he wandered outside to lie upon the grass and be with the earth. He smiled as he surrendered his body. He had heard the call of the earth. He was so connected. It was perfect.

Max is truly an emissary of the universe. He is so connected to both heaven and earth that wherever he goes, the elements dance with joy upon his arrival, for he literally floods the grace of God right down to the ground. Being in Max's field is a privilege.

A few moments later, I knew I was done with my part, and I left his energetic side on the grass. I felt expanded, relaxed, and at peace. Max was resting at peace. The earth was healing him. He was home. He was safe and his heart was free. I no longer worried for him.

In amongst the days, I was living an oscillation between deep spans of emotional and mental pain to expanded realms of blissful healing.

On the 3-D level, my life was continuing to degrade financially, as it seemed that my slate had been cleared for this process. I seemed to have no focus to correct its course. This made no sense to me, but as soon as I would step forward to act on creating, the emotions would mow me over like huge waves in the ocean. The more I tried to make it to shore, the harder they pulled me under and out into deeper seas of struggle. I had to surrender in it and save my strength.

It seemed that it was always Friday—time to set the garbage at the curb. I was getting nothing done, and no amount of discipline would give me focus.

I shared my financial picture with a few close friends and described that I could not imagine how I had gotten there. It felt as though I had been anesthetized and walked to the edge of a cliff, only to wake up and find myself somewhere I had no understanding of. And yet the truth was that I had done it to myself.

My current picture challenged my own inner perception of my character with all the programming that I had around financial net worth equating to character worth. It seemed that no subject area of human definition would be freed from the experience of full annihilation.

Every concept of the 3-D self was being challenged from love to relationships to sex to money to structures, morals, and everything. I was being asked to let go of every single paradigm that veiled the truth of unconditional love and divine creative force. I would be letting it all go.

The morning after I assisted in Mary and Max's energy, I woke feeling the sadness once again. I taught an early morning yoga class, and then took a very lovely couple through a BreathLight experience.

The moment the door closed behind the couple, and I turned to walk toward the kitchen, my body erupted in tears.

"No!" I was so tired of the overwhelming emotion. "Please make it stop!" I begged.

But it was flooding down my face. I made lunch as the tears bounced and splashed, hitting the countertop. I didn't even try to stop them. I tried to ignore them as I pushed myself through the day.

Maybe I need medication, I thought. Maybe I was off balance hormonally or something that could explain this. I felt I needed to think of it all. Surely, no matter what the cause, the effect would show up in blood work. Maybe I needed to see a doctor.

I called my sister and confessed my fears. She assured me that she had checked in so many times with her guidance, and everything that was happening to me was real. I just needed to keep doing what I was doing, and it would all be okay. I was born for this. She was surrounding me with pure love and support, ready to be at my side in a moment's notice.

Angela Ditch

The next afternoon, I got back on the phone with Mary. I needed a progress report from these guides, and I needed some encouragement that I was almost through with the process. I needed some hope.

They didn't even let her finish her opening prayer when they said, "Come back to Sedona." They couldn't emphasize it enough.

The energies in Sedona would support me in this transition, but I could not see a logical way to get there. The entire experience had pulled every opportunity available to physically run, and each time I thought about it, another sign would appear to shut me down.

One day, as I was watering my sister's garden, I walked through her garage to retrieve the hose while having a little temper tantrum in my head.

"I'll run if I fucking want to run!" I stated defiantly. That's when my right-foot sandal broke.

"Seriously?" I said, looking up to the heavens again. "You broke my sandal?"

This was not just a sandal. This was the pair of sandals I had trekked the globe with. They were everywhere, from Kauai to Florida, Costa Rica, Peru, and Canada. For almost one solid year, I never wore any other shoes at all. These represented my mobility in every way. These represented my journey.

I grabbed my truck keys and jumped in, with one sandal on my left foot and the other in my hand. I drove downtown, parked, stepped out, and plugged the meter. I then walked one-footed into the shoe store completely pissed off.

I grabbed the first pair of plain-Jane sandals, paid for them, and tossed the others in the garbage on my way out the door. I didn't even get back into the truck before the tears came.

The universe had asked for everything already. My whole life was different. Now it took my shoes away. I mourned my shoes and felt such shame that I didn't even look back as they hit the bottom of the garbage can. What more could I possibly have to give?

I calmed my emotions and looked into the rearview mirror. Where was I in there? Where was the happy, optimistic, naturally blissed-out being that had resided in this body? Where had she gone?

And this, too, shall pass, I reminded myself. There was something bigger at play here, and I would soon know the answer. In the meantime, I promised I would not run nor joke about it. I didn't want the universe to take away my truck next to top it all off. I would be obedient and get this job done. I would go through it. I would not run, I promised.

Mary finally was able to complete her opening prayer and was continuing into the session. She felt good to begin with, but within seconds, I could feel her energy recoil, and nausea set in for her, so I simply went back into the visualization and held her field to support her. She stabilized instantly and continued into the experience.

I had done well in transmuting old paradigms the guides shared. Under every veil I removed, I always surrendered and found love. And, as the revelations would pour in through every emotional release, I would always discover my true response, and it was always based in unconditional love. I liked me. I liked me a lot. I was love at the core of my soul.

The guides said that I had mastered this realm of process, and I was literally hanging above the great void by one tiny thread of light. They asked me to imagine my outstretched hand hanging from a rope that had now frayed down to one tiny minute thread.

They explained that this thread was a continuity that extended through every single incarnation I had ever had, from the very beginning of the universe itself. This last filament of droplets of light represented the one thing I had sought in every existence. It was love. I was hanging onto the longing for the deepest love. I was hanging on for pure true divine union.

The thread was Max. Max had been in every one of my lives right from the beginning of time. He was the constant. That is why I jumped so fearlessly into his eyes in an invitation that never ended. It would be the only reason I would have made this leap and have accepted this mission.

They kept repeating, "You leapt for love, Angela. This was the plan from the start of time."

This final filament of light that extended through every lifetime was the last piece of human self-identity. They wanted me to know that the next and final step was to let it go.

I cried nonstop throughout the session. They kept saying that this was not an external action in my physical world. It was an internal surrender in my whole being. I would be letting go of the human self entirely and all the lifetimes strung together in the quest to find him and re-merge into one.

In the letting go, I would dissolve the human ego and embody the divine grace of the feminine fully. I would wake the goddess in the cells and tissues of this living form.

My human body-mind wept with grief. This was what was happening. I was grieving myself, my own personality death. That is why the separation was so intense. It wasn't just about the love of this amazing man. This was about letting go of my human self.

I didn't know how to even do this. I had to trust that it would all just happen.

Did it mean that I would never see Max again in his physical realm? Was this asking me to let him go here and now when he had just found me? How could this be asked of me? Is this why he was married? Is this why he was in another dimension? Is this why we could not be fully unified in all realms of spiritual, mental, emotional, etheric, and physical?

How could the universe tease me like this? He was the bait to get me to this edge. It was perfect. I mean, really, we all think we want spiritual enlightenment, but we have no idea what that asks of the human self.

My human self was being asked to die to a new experience, and, as much as my soul yearned to hear its splash merging into the oneness of the great void, my body-mind felt so sad.

They called it primal terror. They assured me that it was not personal. It was not mine. It was not my cellular, ancestral, or past life terror to transmute. This would be the entire human race's collective terror. This would be the last human request of me. After that, I would be released from the pain.

They talked of a joy that is indescribable awaiting me. All I had to do was let go. They told me that I would know how to do that. I just needed to go within to find the answer for myself.

Mary was so compassionate. She told me that she was instructed to keep an eye on me, and that we would need to talk within three days again. I thanked her and concluded the call, and then I cried many tears into the night.

As I lay in my bed, emptying an entire box of Kleenex, a peace and surrender was setting in. I would just let him go. I would just let him go back to his life, and I would sit in gratitude for the catalyst that he had stepped up to be. I would just simply let it all go.

The guides spoke to the depth of the feminine story when they painted the picture that he had failed to show up to meet me in that beautiful merge. But the truth was that he showed up perfectly to launch me into the truest dive of all. I was merging into me. I was going to find me in all of this, my truest of essence, the purest of loves, the holiest of holies. I would find true self as I surrendered the ego, letting go of this final thread.

Chapter 24

The next morning I woke feeling Max at the portal. When I walked through the entrance he was standing under the tree waiting for me with a latte in his hand. He dreamt he had lost me and he refused to believe it was so. I shared pieces of my experiences, and we remerged back into that beautiful, surrendered, honest state of communication. Our eyes did most of the talking, and our bodies just relaxed in the comfort of knowing who we were to one another. Acknowledging the truth and scope of our connection took pain away immediately.

We sat on the grass, silently, leaning our backs against the tree, in a state of blissful surrender. It was time to just let go. Even though I knew not how to do this, time and space were the only answer. We both knew this and we both knew that this was not the end; it was just the now, the now in a connection that knew no end.

In the scheme of eternity, this was but a fraction of a second in time, and the more we held the presence of that truth, the deeper we could penetrate it into the illusion. Our faith in our connection was opening up the deepest shadows to the full light of unconditional love.

We had to face realities. We could not be together. He was married. I had to remove my energy from his sphere so he could be fully present with his wife. It was not fair to anyone to let it continue this way. The physical attraction was not lessening, it was growing stronger. The suppression was not healthy and yet there was no alternative in sight.

I needed time away to give me the space to figure out what it meant to let go, to let go in absolutely every sense of the word. No longer did I cling to the idea that my purpose was to hold the portal open. I would surrender that.

Maybe I would be leaving the area again. I did not know. I let all plans dissolve. I gave everything back to the universe to wait for the clearest impulse. I would not challenge roadblocks; I would accept them as guidance to keep surrendering.

As we leaned our backs against the tree trunk in the courtyard, I wondered what Adam and Eve would do if given the chance to take all this knowledge into their choice. How would they unify the now created polarity belief in separation? How would they truly repair the split or evolve beyond its painful perpetual cyclical nature?

The light had faded and darkness was setting in as I rose to my feet to leave the courtyard. Max stood and struck a match to light the lantern that sat upon the table. He smiled with such confidence and said, "I will keep the lantern lit for you Angela, so you can find your way home to me. Don't worry. There is a reason for all of this. God doesn't make mistakes."

I smiled, surrendered in my heart. Even though I missed him already, there was such comfort in knowing that nothing could ever take us apart. We were one essence shining through two bodies, in entirely different dimensions and still we could find each other. I felt such faith as I slipped back through the portal and set myself to finish the job.

I began to let go of everything. I began to examine the creation I was in the middle of with a new sense of objective perspective. His energy relaxed, mine relaxed, and I could feel him at a whole new expansive level. Everything calmed, and the creativity in me rose. The book was suddenly ready to be birthed. It made me very happy, as it prompted me to get my computer and type.

The emotional waves calmed, and the waters began to still. The pain in his body subsided. A sense of peace came with a deeper sense of appreciation for all that I had taken for granted in my life in those moments of true bliss. I had no idea what it was like to be depressed like this. I took my optimism for granted, but now I had compassion for those who transmute these energies. I had no idea what they went through.

Most of my life had been an oscillation from one extreme to the other. I was always seeking balance. Embarking on my self-guided journey had taught me how to witness it all and find peace at the zero point.

Max's arrival swung me so far into the elevated and expanded bliss of union that the pendulum had no choice but to swing as hard and far toward the pain of separation to balance it. They were each other's polarity.

A few days later, into my e-mail inbox came a link to an article found online. Its title was "The Stages of a Twin-Flame Relationship." Did I want to read it? I had such an aversion to the concept of fairy tales. Would this be one? I avoided it for a couple of hours, and then finally made a cup of tea and opened it.

Here it is in increments. It was too perfect to paraphrase, so I give credit to Jenna Forest off the profoundhealingforsensitives.com website.

The Stages of a Twin-Flame Relationship

Stage 1. Recognition and Temporary Spiritual Awakening

Both twins recognize one another at the soul level and feel as if they have met before. Synchronous events surround the union, the heart chakra opens and both souls quickly merge into a third unified energy. Both twins experience an acceleration of spiritual understanding.

(The Purpose of the Recognition Stage & Temporary Awakenings Stage: To activate the memory of each soul's life mission and to help awaken each twin to higher levels of consciousness.)

It was true. I knew him the moment he walked around the counter in that coffee shop. He had paced the park the moment he found my book. Neither of us knew what or why, but we followed a tractor beam that pulled us together through time and space. Within seconds of being in the same physical realm, the visions and knowing flooded in for both of us. We could amp each other up on every level merely on the thought of one another.

Stage 2. Testing

The initial temporary spiritual awakening (illumination) fades. The ego (little self) begins to reemerge. One or both twins may attempt to fit the relationship into the "old model" of love, couple hood and relationship as it relates to their ego desires and learned false beliefs. Inner conflict arises. Twins ruminate on what they were taught to believe their beloved "should be" and how relationships are supposed to serve them. Both twins feel simultaneously inspired and toppled by power of the union. Doubts creep in, making one or both twins begin to view their beloved critically or suspiciously.

(The Purpose of the Testing Stage: To cause outdated mental concepts about relationships to rise to the surface to be cleared.)

The fact that he was married brought up so much conflict internally as we sought to acknowledge the truth of who we were while denying the impulses that naturally arose. 3-D paradigms of relationship were being dissolved in the light of the truest of unconditional cosmic loves. No longer did the old paradigms make sense in the face of something so real and pure.

Stage 3. Crisis

The crisis of the twin is realizing they must either reject egoic beliefs about love relationships or reject their beloved. Having to shed "little self" or identity based beliefs and desires to embrace a higher expression of love can lead to stubbornness and anxiety. Fear can take hold, triggering many habitual dysfunctional emotional patterns. In staying present with the patterns, they can be witnessed and released. Despite fears, both twins naturally come together in cycles for bonding, confession, forgiveness, and lovemaking. These rituals cement higher levels of consciousness into the energy fields of both twins.

(The Purpose of the Crisis Stage: To provide opportunities for healing and maturing of mental and emotional bodies.)

The natural flow of the creative energy was flooding through us within a field becoming distorted by our attempts to repress and deny it. It began to create nothing but difficulty and roadblocks. We had ignited an atomic bomb of creative energy, and without a navigation system it flew around chaotically, messing everything up.

All the while, I kept discovering that I didn't fit the norms of structure when it came to love, sex, and relationship. This both freed me and scared me as I began to dissolve all man-made boundaries regarding Max.

Stage 4. Runner Dynamic

The human spirit naturally fears annihilation in the face of the divine unified consciousness encoded inside the twin flame union. The pain body rises up and old ego survival mechanisms or "bottom of the barrel" emotional and mental patterns like defiance, resistance, manipulation, anger, punishing, and judgment arise. One or both twins become emotionally and mentally flooded with deep pain from what feels like a soul level, rejection and abandonment. The unbearable soul level pain leads one or both twins to withdraw physically and block communication in fear and futility. One or both twins may also unsuccessfully try to re-create the original unified harmony.

(The Purpose of the Runner Dynamic: To propel both individuals toward God for healing and maturation of the spiritual body.)

By the time the pain came into the picture with Max's injury, the collective illusions were lined up to be cleared, and our bodies became the portals of unity for them. If we had been clear and prepared ourselves, we would have transmuted them through simple presence, but this task now called for personal transmutation through the body, emotions, and mind. It was crucifixion on every level for both of us as we held space for millennia of trapped emotions of separation, destined to be freed into new potentials.

Stage 5. Surrender

The direction and outcome of the relationship is surrendered to God in full faith and trust that the union is under divine protection. It is accepted that what is best and destined for the final physical harmonization will conspire in its own time. (Both twins must reach illumination in order to harmonize in the physical) The "runner" twin is allowed the space and freedom to choose to evolve at their own pace in their own way.

At this stage, the frequency of compassion returns and maintains itself. The surrendered twin holds a heart space for their beloved while fully exploring life on way to becoming an illuminated human. This may be a time of channeling unconditional love into art, music, writing, teaching, active service or some other creative outlet.

(Purpose of the Surrender Phase: To help each soul release the ego, develop regular communication with God and demonstrate their full trust in God to do what is best and when.)

Surrender came with such grace. My heart was bowed to the ground to release all the templates of human programming around love, sex, relationship, and money. When you have nothing else to hold onto, stopping the grasp to hold on is given. This wasn't letting go; it was simply surrender to a higher power of trust. As Max continuously stated, "God doesn't make mistakes, Angela. There is a reason for this. Please don't run away."

Stage 6. Self-Realization, Illumination and Radiance

The ego or little self-dies and God-force energy takes over. This leads to a complete spiritual awakening, arriving at one's fully awakened divinity. This is the stage of radiating divine love rather than seeking romantic love. At this stage, the surrendered twin's emotional, mental, spiritual bodies arrive at full maturity. New creativity and healing abilities arise, which are put in service to assist others.

(Purpose of the Radiance Stage: To establish an outward flow of divine love through one's body and works, which vibrates at a level that uplifts humanity.)

The energy of the transmuting polarities was creating a field of creativity and healing so immense that it gave great scope and purpose to everything. The book was pouring through, and the energetic field of healing energy was precise and clear. It made everything so meaningful, and, once again, a higher purpose was visible.

Stage 7. Harmonizing

By this stage, both twins have awakened. They come together in the physical to assimilate their newly evolved energies, flowing into a new dynamic of their unified potential. Both twins integrate fully into the third energy of unconditional love in a way that influences others towards their own heart opening.

(Purpose of the Harmonization Phase: To fulfill the intended mission of the Twin Flame union. Twin Flame Relationships come into your life to help mold you to embody the vibration of unconditional love.)"

How perfect were these words. There I sat, predominantly in surrender, having been coached to see and dip my toes in the next two stages before me. I felt peace. The peace came from the knowing that this was exactly what was taking place. I felt peace in the knowing that this would be of benefit to many. I felt gratitude to have been given such a powerful catalyst for awakening.

All that I believed about this man and me in our connection was so beautifully articulated for the truth of what was happening for us. I could relax in the knowing that I could trust my perceptions and breathe relief in knowing what we had already passed through.

As I stepped out of the shower the next morning, written into the steam on the mirror, was a note that simply said, "Did you enjoy my email?" Somehow Max had e-mailed the article to me himself. He knew the truth. We were twins separated from the beginning of time.

Nothing would change who we were to each other, and who we were to each other required no set physical form. Yes, there would always be the pull to merge on every level, but, as the final stages of our evolution would transpire, we would once again rest in the original heights of the connection. It was simply cosmic universal love in oneness.

We had come together to launch each other into an illuminated, embodied service to humanity. We knew this from the start; we just had no idea what that meant. I have so much gratitude, and I am deeply humbled. And I have so much compassion for our body-minds and what they have been through.

I understand now why my soul walked me to the edge of financial pressure. I would have run away every day, multiple times, if the means had been available. I knew this. The crucible, as the guides described it, was created to hold me in place to get the job done and to learn even deeper lessons that were coming.

Even my friend Marcia pointed out to me the perfection of my sandal breaking while I taunted the guidance. It illustrated how perfectly it was all playing out. The sandals had faithfully walked me to the full realization that it was time to stop running away.

Max was ready all along. He had shown up perfectly and played exactly the role intended. He wasn't meant to arrive in 3-D and catch me. The truth was coming through. He opened the portal for my ascension and he extended his hand out to reach me. He showed up to rescue me from the illusion.

Sometimes these relationships are not destined for the physical experience of merging. Sometimes the amplification of the senses is meant to pull the activation deep into embodiment. Sometimes the energies are designed to merge at the higher levels and be offered up to the community as a transmission of pure embodied bliss.

This is why he came in married. This is why he stayed in the higher dimension. If he had not, we would have merged in 3-D and played out the process in traditional relationship. By having these boundaries, it launched us into the universal service and sent us toward the ultimate divine union, union with pure true essence of self.

Collective service was our mission, and someday, when we were ready, we would be able to amplify the field together in practices we saw from the start. Our awakened selves would energetically merge and broadcast a transmission that would guide others to awaken to their true selves in a divine union that existed beyond the illusion of separation.

I had faith that the divine God Source had it all worked out, and that it was being protected and guided in its perfect timing. Here we were, only months into our current lifetime connection, and look how far we'd come. It was mind-blowing.

In the meantime, my task at hand was to figure out how to truly let go of that final thread of human self-connection, the thread that embarked me on an eternal search for divine union in love in the first place. The thread that had me search the cosmos for Max, my twin resonating energy.

He had found me. He breathed. Now I was going to understand the true gift of what he was truly giving me. Now I would learn what it meant to let go.

Chapter 25

I went through the Starbucks lineup and ordered my usual venti nonfat latte. Lately it seemed that all great revelations came with a coffee in my hand. I would review all that I had learned and see what gems of wisdom would reveal themselves in the process. Soon it would all make sense and I would find a way to embody the knowing.

When the guides spoke about my letting the thread go, they clearly said that this was not something to do in my physical world, it was an adjustment to be made in my internal world. All my experience and teachings thus far led me to the clear understanding that what was happening in my outside world was merely a projection of my inside world. As above, so below. As within, so without.

In many ways the body is simply a sophisticated projection lens. Imagine that your spine is a tube through which the light of the cosmos shines. As the light travels through the tube, it is bent and adjusted based on your own unique alignment. When the light shines out through the lens, it echoes out a sound current that travels into the great void of infinite potential and gathers up all the elements needed to create a three-dimensional hologram of your expression. This is the mechanics of the law of attraction. What you put out is what you get back, amplified.

The alignment of the tube is determined by your overall distilled attitude. Attitude is comprised of thoughts, emotions, intentions and postures. Postures form through a history of experience that is collected and stored within the crystalline structure of the tissues of the body. What does it smell like, taste like, look like, feel like and sound like is being recorded 24/7 by a sensory system that never quits.

This database of experience is then framed into generalized rules or programs that the autopilot system of the body-mind then uses for immediate reaction when a familiar sensory experience returns.

To understand how the lens is set, one can simply look at the outside world picture to see what one is attracting and creating. What one is attracting and creating is what one is being. It is a perfect mirror.

Look at my current experience. I had been attracting the most epic connections, intensifying in succession, and each was either unavailable or temporary in nature. What did that tell me?

It told me that I was operating at an increasingly epic level of openness while being unavailable and temporary. As within, so without.

Each experience was precipitated by the intention of having the deepest, most authentic merge to experience true divine union and unconditional love. Each experience was resulting in the reinforcement that I was not worthy of having the complete union.

I would find a beautiful mirror of depth and love, but the merging wasn't taking place. Somewhere within me I didn't believe I deserved the full experience.

Once I honed my request, and asked for the deepest, most authentic, never-ending dive, the universe brought me an experience that I could no longer run away from or avoid. I was forced to face deep personal, ancestral and collective illusions of being separated and forsaken. I was forced to clear the energetics trapped within the literal physical tissues of my own body, and within the collective conscious belief systems within the field of unity itself.

I was trained for it. Everything up to that moment was merely preparation for where I had been heading my whole life.

I had spent years studying all the rudimentary concepts that would lead me to this understanding of myself. I used yoga and meditation to begin the observation process of what was arising within me, so that I could consciously adjust the autopilot programs. I used the postures in yoga to literally pool energy and flood it through the tissues to release the programming from the body itself.

I used breath practices to open the pathways of energy flow and blast them with prana to activate kundalini, raising my consciousness as the energy cleared the chakra system. I used dance to become more fluid in my movement and bring my body into one unified whole, rather than a collection of body parts attached at the joints. I used sound current through chanting and singing to vibrate sacred frequencies within my brain, spinal fluid, and cellular tissues to attune to higher octaves of awareness.

All of these strengthened my nervous system and glandular system, so I could run increasing amounts of energy in elevating frequencies with greater ease. All of these had blasted my body open to receive more light and project a frequency that would attract epic, deep connections.

I used plant medicines to expand my perceptions. I used neuro-biofeedback brain training to clear stuck patterns in my nervous system. I used Vipassana meditation to examine and hold space for every square inch of my body.

All was complimented by white tantric meditations—deep, energetic clearing practices done with partners in groups. One day of white tantra is said to be equivalent in energy clearing to one hundred kundalini yoga classes. I'd done nine days of tantra already.

I'd been through four thirty-day kundalini immersion intensives. I had travelled and touched the lands and ruins of many sacred sites, and now I'd done Explosive Sexual Healing to awaken and open the sexual creative circuits in my body.

My channel was ready to run. I had let go of everything imaginable. I reviewed and challenged every belief pertaining to love, sex, relationship, and money. Now it was the thread. Everything in my life was leading to this thread.

I felt I was getting close, and I felt faith. Faith was unwavering now, and this was comforting. I just had to trust that as my fingers typed on the keyboard, the book would answer the questions. And that is exactly what happened.

I suddenly remembered all my mathematical training. In order to let something go, you would have to zero it; hence, the zero-point perspective is the place of infinite creative potential with no form. Let's look at this as an equation. After all, mathematics is the universal language.

If unity and separation were opposites, then adding them together would equal zero. As 1 and -1 are opposite, when you add them together, you get zero. In order to cancel out the thread, I would have to add it's opposite to it in an equation. Stay with me.

If you took a thread that had separation on the bottom and union on the top, and you then took a second identical thread and flipped it, placing polar opposites together, they would cancel each other out. This represented the joining of masculine and feminine polarities.

And if you thought about it for a moment, inside the spinal column, two channels, one masculine and one feminine, spiraled in a dance around the central channel of unity, up the spine, to join from the root chakra all the way to the third eye chakra.

This explained what happened when Max's energy field and my energy field merged. The twin energy in polar reflection created a zero point of infinite perpetual energy. Our fields would literally combine and begin to circulate in an ever-increasing amped up perpetual flow of unity.

I liked the logic. It made sense. I always enjoyed math in school, and especially loved using it to solve problems. But the real problem was that Max and I didn't have the option to truly connect this way.

I paced the floor while I made a tea, knowing there was more to come, and then the picture came flooding into my head as I heard the repeating advice that letting go would come from my inside world, not my outside world.

All of the lifetimes of longing and questing for unity had been directed toward the form of the external. What if I took the separation end of the thread and brought it together with the union side of the thread in a circle? That would be internal, and surely, that would cancel them out. That's when I saw the ancient symbol of the ouroboros, the serpent that swallows its own tail.

Floods of knowing came pouring in. Not only was this a good idea, but also the actual act of taking a thread and placing the ends together created a zero. How obvious!

Ouroboros represents cyclical creation. It is the depiction of something recreating itself perpetually, a primordial unity. Of course! Of course!

It made sense. I had seen this symbol many times in my journeys to sacred sites. Okay, this was it. I would have to find a way to merge unity and separation together within myself.

Holding the zero-point perspective as things arose in my awareness was easy now. I would simply stay neutral and let the effects of the experience be felt and released. This didn't really cancel out the bigger polarity, but it taught me to keep a balance and clear deeper programs within the body. It also got me through the intensity of all the soul-level pain and trapped collective emotion I was transmuting with Max.

This would be the same but different. If Max and I had actually had the opportunity to connect, our physical bodies would have formed the circuit of union and helped to cancel each other out by our sheer polarity of masculine and feminine. As perfect opposites in twin energy, we clicked together like a set, and even without physical contact, our energy connected in the circular perpetual motion of primordial union.

Our perfect connection makes it impossible not to initiate this, unless a tremendous amount of contraction and avoidance is applied through the lens of our bodies. If we had allowed the energy to continue to amp and escalate through physical contact, we may have cleared everything. But, as we are reminded, things were perfectly orchestrated for a reason, and the biggest piece was that he came in married.

Transmuting the polarity and its illusions was not meant to occur this way. We were meant to do it on our own. The reason why was becoming clearer and clearer.

This was about divine union within. This was about unconditionally loving ourselves separately. My mind groaned! "Seriously? Love yourself? This is the answer to this experience?"

We all know that we need to love ourselves first, but that statement has become the most popular new-age bumper sticker and carries the meaning of autospeak. So, seriously, what does it mean in practical terms to love yourself?

Asking the questions seemed to be the only thing necessary for the answers to arrive. Ask and you shall receive. It was truly that simple.

I was driving to my sister's to water her garden, and when I got a block away from my house, I realized that I had forgotten my earbuds for my iPhone. I like to listen to beautiful music when I water for her, and after realizing I had forgotten them, I simply thought, *Oh well, I can do without them today.*

That's when I realized that if anyone else had been in the vehicle, and it were their earbuds that were left behind, I would have turned the truck around immediately. I would have wanted them to have what they needed in order to have the best experience. So why would I not do it for me? I immediately turned around and got my earbuds.

This was how it was. I would shortchange my own comfort, desire, and needs at every turn. I ate simply rather than create a meal of something I loved, but if someone else were coming over, I would cook.

It was in the simplest of things I would do. My habit was to deprioritize anything that required effort for my own sake. I did the minimal required to make myself comfortable at home, and I would procrastinate on things that would make my life run more smoothly.

Why? Was I lazy? No. When I truly needed or wanted to get something done, I just did it, and I did it wholeheartedly and with passion. So, if I wasn't lazy, what was the true root of my lack of placing a priority around taking care of myself?

It was a core belief that I was not loveable. In order to hold that belief, I had put myself last on the list and would neglect my own wants over the wants or needs of others.

Everywhere I turned, I could see where I was not really loving myself in the simplest of ways. Yes, I had changed so many things in my life and had taken exceptional strides to be happier. I had done an immense amount of self-realization work that brought great understanding and acceptance of myself. I saw patterns clearly and did much to release them. Yet, I still operated on a primal belief that I was not loveable, which came right from the separation end of the thread. Therefore, I continuously found ways to demonstrate it to myself and to the world around me.

As within, so without. And there I had the perfect recipe for "unavailable and temporary." I literally projected the energetic that I was not worthy. Ouch!

It was time to do the obvious. I would love myself the way I loved him. I would look in the mirror with full presence and fall into my own eyes with such love and tenderness that I would support my whole self in every endeavor. The transmuting of all the pain kept showing me the same thing. Underneath every veil of illusion, I was unconditional love and I liked me. I would now see the best in me and encourage me through positive support.

I would rise each day to see how I could serve myself in my health and happiness. I would make yummy food with love and creativity and take the time to serve it to myself as though I were a most honored guest at the table. I would clean my space and keep it sacred, so that my whole essence would feel like royalty.

I would ensure I got beautiful rest and spent time laughing and enjoying friendships and connections that built wonderful templates of community. I would look after my own happiness needs, and then overflow into the community with a healthy frequency that would amp up the whole space even more. In my example, I would invite everyone else to do the same.

I would care for my body with exercise, loving touch, and nurturing, so that my temple stayed honored and healthy for me to express through. I would build energy through practice and mindfulness. I would look at myself like I was the most beautiful woman in the world. I would love myself the way he would love me.

But most of all, I would be present with me. Instead of shoveling spoonfuls of oatmeal into my mouth as I checked e-mails and thought about the laundry needing to be switched from the washer to the dryer, I would savor the cinnamon flavor of warmth on my tongue. I would give myself my full undivided honoring and loving presence, just as I would do for every soul who came into my circle. I would extend the prayer and gratitude I offered for my food to the very breath that entered my body. Just typing the words was changing everything.

Realizations were flooding in through a continuous flow. I no longer could avoid seeing where I was unloving to myself. All my programming to take care of myself had seemed like an arduous effort to be procrastinated to the next day or disciplined through the continuous pulse of the "should" word. It came from the illusion of not being loveable that naturally resided at the opposite end of divine union love.

But here was the biggest realization of all. I wasn't defectively programmed as my mind believed. This wasn't something to repattern as I'd tried diligently to do. This wasn't the result of bad parenting or past-life memories. I wasn't filled with blocks nor was the world around me. I was simply human.

Humans balance polar opposites in every moment of their lives. They do it for themselves, and they do it for the collective. We are in a continuous state of reconciling the split. It is what being human means.

I simply was in a constant state of balancing all polarity as every—I repeat—*every* human does when you attempt to do it from the linear view of the thread with two ends—from the internal to the external.

All along I sought the completion of myself, the validation of my worth and the measure of my lovability from sources outside of myself in my own hologram. Only the projection I broadcast didn't contain the necessary information to create what I desired.

The program of being unlovable simply served as the slingshot force that pulled the thread back and created the momentum to shoot toward being loveable. The whole model was becoming so simple. Instead of allowing the momentum to shoot me toward the outer world, looking for love from another, I would loop it back, like the ouroboros swallowing its own tail, and direct the momentum inward. And how beautiful the result would be as that momentum then created a perpetual motion of energy that only the zero point can achieve.

The polarity was always going to have momentum. The polarity would always exist in human form. Looping it back upon itself—as the serpent swallowing its own tail—simply created an unending circuit of unity, primordial unity.

Max easily represented both ends of the polarity and the lure to attract me to union. As separated twins, Max and I were sent on a cosmic search for each other. If we were to truly find the union, we would have to dissolve the illusions of human experience; otherwise, we would continuously oscillate back and forth between union and separation, in our external world, as we played out the human game of duality along the thread it created.

With the intensity of our connection and the limitation created by him being married, the swings were proving to be immensely wide, spanning from absolute bliss to intense soul-level pain. If we did not unify this within ourselves first, this oscillation would never be broken.

This epic, blissful, tragic experience Max and I were having had been perfectly orchestrated in absolutely every way. I now understood exactly how I would zero the thread.

Chapter 26

More revelations came. The chair in France, diversely known as the Seat of Isis and the Devil's Armchair, was the perfect depiction of one ascending the realms of the duality ladder by bringing all three energy lay-lines into a unified point that would channel into one holistic self.

The Body Ascension Map, as shown in one perspective of the Bible's story, described the journey of balancing the polarities within the chakra themes to ascend the ladder to the third eye and choose separation or unity.

Adam and Eve chose separation by identifying with, and focusing on, their differences, forming judgment and aversion. Then they journeyed through the cycles of reincarnation as the human species began its ascent back into unity consciousness.

Jesus chose unity, then transmuted the polarity through his body, and then ascended with the body to a heavenly realm beyond the earth.

Each was presented with the challenge of the superego through the arrival of Satan and the choice to choose the perspective of either the Seat of Isis (unity) or the Devil's Armchair (separation).

In a lot of ways it's like an elaborate ride at the amusement park. One tube takes you downward in the game of separation. One tube takes you to the ascension of unity. But the most important discovery is that there is a next level of the game and to access it you need do only one thing – upgrade the operating system of your human body-mind.

Search the database of your mind and wherever you find the concept of OR, replace it with AND.

You are not separate OR unified. You are separate AND unified. Each one of us is merely a fractal expression of the whole. You are not finite OR infinite. You are finite AND infinite. You do not experience pain OR pleasure. You experience pain AND pleasure. And you are not a body OR a soul. You are a body AND a soul.

The circuit that runs within the spine that splits the polarity is connected at both the root and the third eye, therefore the ascension of your consciousness is not beyond the body but is contained within the body itself.

The body is not a trap of flesh that must be denied. The ego choice of separation is the trap. The swinging of the polarities is the trap. The concept of OR is the trap. The body is the temple of form that your consciousness has created in order to experience this incredible human ride. It is your Avatar! You are a soul AND a body. Unify them! Connect the circuit within the spine.

There is more. In the story of Jesus, we are told that he is "the way, the truth and the life" and that all who achieve ascension will do so through him.

So what did he represent? He stood for truth, dealing with what is, as it is, free of judgment or aversion. Teach your body-mind to love and accept what is and you will inspire a world of shift within you.

He stood for compassion. Walking your own path is not always easy, nor is the path of another. Having compassion for all we go through is the first step to truly loving yourself and then to unconditionally loving others.

The most impactful thing, in my opinion, is that he stood for forgiveness. I'll be honest; I didn't truly understand the concept of forgiveness until about a month before I typed this paragraph.

In my life I had decided acceptance was all that was needed. What was there to forgive anyway? I would accept that what I had created was busy echoing out of my field only to return as a consequence of karma. I felt I would get what I deserved and that would be that.

Then one day, as I felt the presence of a great master standing behind me, forgiveness rippled through my body like a field of its own frequency and I finally understood. Forgiveness accepts the truth of what is and what has been, and then, with compassion, it sends a neutralizing wave to release the echoing return of the karmic seeds, dissolving them into new potentials and possibilities. Forgiveness changes the future by cancelling out the echo coming back.

This would be the way to the next level of the game. Right now we are in a cyclical perpetual creation of the same thing over and over and over again. This is happening by sheer evolution of multitudes of echoes coming back to interact and evolve us along our path.

As the feminine polarity we are the seedbed of creation. The masculine is the seed of consciousness and the feminine is the soil of form. If the feminine polarity could forgive, the entire landscape of human experience would change immediately.

Continuing from the same analogy of the story of Adam and Eve, if Eve, the feminine polarity, could forgive herself for the choice of the separation - if she could stop blaming herself and stop choosing to see herself as less worthy and of deserving punishment - if she could stop seeking validation and love from outside of herself, she would no longer be unequal in her own creation.

If she could forgive Adam for denying her and forsaking her in her hours of most need - if she could forgive the millennia of mistreatment of the feminine side of the species - if she could do all of this, truly, deeply within her very cells, she would neutralize all the incoming echoes of perpetuation of these cycles. She would create a seedbed into which these concepts were simply unknown.

And if she could hold a genuine field of unconditional love for the divine masculine, a field filled with trust and faith and receptivity, he would return surrendered, reverent and graceful into the bosom of her warmth, honoring and protecting her sacred nature.

This is the work of the Goddess. This is how she wakes. Within her very body, lie the channels through which creation blooms into form. She is the holder of the template and the moment she can no longer conceive of a world of disunity, is the moment it will no longer exist.

It is exactly the words that Jesus spoke upon that cross, as he looked to those who had put him there, when he said, "Forgive them Father, for they know not what they do."

Can you feel it? Can you feel that frequency of dissolution of all the incoming echoes of the illusion?

If we unify the polarity at the third eye, and accept the divinity of the body at the root chakra, then the circuit will be complete within us, and the body-mind will evolve to the next level of the game. First, it will surrender its false illusion of control. To do this, it will be taught to function in this spherical ouroboros unifying pattern, rather than through linear balancing of opposites, seeking connection from outside of self.

The body-mind will be taught to simultaneously see all perspectives at once. It will see both ends of each thread at the same time and bring them together, understanding the cause and effect in the same moment. This is the true zero-point perspective. It is like sitting in the middle of a ball and seeing the entire surface and its contents all at once.

This allows for the conscious selection of the seeds that would be planted and tended. With instantaneous understanding of the full result of the cause and effect, all unwanted seeds would be cancelled by immediate acceptance, compassion and forgiveness.

As I sat typing these words, a sensation I can only describe as a brain orgasm was happening within the back and upper part of my head. Floods of expanding circles of energy were moving like jellyfish swimming. Fully formed toroidal concepts were pulsing in my brain like bubbles bursting with wisdom. I had to stop typing and just feel it.

The joy bursting through my cells as I typed those words was indescribable. A sense of wholeness overcame me, and I could feel multiple points of awareness at the same time, like each was simultaneously the core focus of my attention.

Instead of balancing negative and positive elements, I was merging a whole sphere of awareness into one zero-point perspective. Instead of reacting to a swing and awaiting the delivery of the consequence in my outer world, I was assessing the entire implication all at once as the seed was coming into form. Through this perspective, pure awareness, acceptance, compassion and unconditional love allowed for the choice to forgive the seed or to plant it.

How funny. Zero Point Perspectives had been my website name for five years. I got the name in a download, along with the message that I would grow to understand its ever-expanding meaning.

I used to think of it like the zero on a linear numerical scale, where the numbers went off in negatives on one side and positives on the other side.

First, I trained myself to identify which side of the scale my thoughts and emotions fell, then I would learn to stand and observe this from the zero point with no judgment. By doing so, the charge of the imbalance would come back to that middle path of neutrality.

It was a continuous conscious balancing with some moments stationed, resting at the pure peace of the zero.

Then it became a merry-go-round, and if I were to jump on and stay at the outer edge, I would feel a force wanting to toss me off the side as I struggled to grip. But if I walked to the center of the spin at the zero point, I could stand hands free and see the ride 360 degrees all around me as I spun.

Now my brain literally built a platform within my skull just at the back of the pineal and slightly above. My neck and brain stem had been activated and feeling like they were enlarging for weeks. Now I knew why.

The hemispheres of my brain were being altered by the energetics running through me, and the conceptual upgrade of a whole new operating system, initially downloaded in the December 2012 galactic sun alignment, was now being activated and coming online.

The split unity energy literally ran up the spine of the physical body, feeding separate hemispheres of the brain, to drive a highly sophisticated biomechanical lens of expansion and contraction toward the quest of balance.

The continuous choices made to expand or contract left us wriggling through time and space like tadpoles in our evolution.

No human could stay on one side of the polarity. It is impossible. One could find the balance point at the zero and float along effortlessly. But now all of this was changing.

The evolution of our species is changing the entire way we function and this has been initiated by a whole new operating system and the simple command of "replace OR with AND."

We are going to bend the linear ends of the thread of polarity and merge them into a circle like the ouroboros serpent swallowing its own tail. And in a 3-D view, we are going to exist within the center of a sphere. Our awareness will move from two points of awareness to all points of awareness, understanding all the implications at once. Our point of navigation will come from the seat at the center of this gyroscopic perception, in the true zero point of perpetual infinite possibility and motion. We are moving into true live streaming creation.

From this new perspective, we will pulse, consciously, the distilled essence of our true self out into the void of infinite potential. We will edit the auto-pilot seeding of karmas through awareness, love, acceptance, compassion and forgiveness. We will nurture and flourish the desired seeds through the magic of our sensual creative channels, honoring the natural flows as sacred. We will consciously create pure unity through acceptance of the whole.

I could feel it in my brain. Pressure in my neck connecting the heart and mind was constant, and it left me feeling like I was being stretched from the inside out to create a larger pathway.

The four points of main awareness in my head lit up. The occipital at the back of the skull, pineal at the center of the brain, eyebrow center, and crown of the head were in constant sensation. Now my ears were more receptive. My skin felt a heightened sense of touch. Smells were calling my awareness, sounds of high-pitched radio frequencies were audible, and the third-eye visions were popping in clarity. Every experience was being tasted with full sensual presence, just as in the moment that the energy ignited Max and I. It was full sensual primal activation as the circuit not only connected at the third eye, but also at the base of the spine, deep in the primal instincts of my physical avatar.

A pressure at the back of the pineal gland area lit up a platform that extended from this point across the roof of my mouth to resemble an energetic drum skin pulled taut and vibrating. The vibrations moved into my brain fluid, creating sounds that tuned all the cells, pulsing down through the spinal cord to broadcast the new programming out amongst the nerve pathways, mutating cells and tissues with the new information.

Then little surges of sensation, like toroidal bubbles rising in water, began to emit from this point just behind the pineal gland, bursting like transmissions of awareness that echo outward, returning what is emitted with ease.

Sensations that travelled across and deep within my brain resulted in blissful activations, filling me with joy beyond my wildest imaginings. Sensory upgrades of perception expanded to every part of my body and every sense all at the same time.

There I sat in the cool basement of Rae-Lynne's beautiful home on that warm summer evening, perched upon a pillow on my yoga mat, with my laptop upon my knee. My mouth was agape as the expansions and awareness came and knew no end. Gratitude and joy became me.

Every being in my life had contributed to the perfection of this very moment, every experience, and every interaction. Within this new spherical perception, I could sense it all at once. I had swung so wide in both directions of this polarity, this human experience, that I understood the collective pain and joy.

The expanses I could now reach were made possible by transmuting the illusions through this very body. They gave me access to the collective in a way that never finds an edge. I simply merged into my surroundings with no boundaries, through a field of truth and love, within the sea of creative magic itself.

Before, when I would meet a block or shadowy illusion, I would retract like a high-speed tape measurer and run away, certain I had breached boundaries. Convinced I was unworthy and unlovable, I behaved with shame like a spectator in the world as I searched for the deepest of connection to validate my existence. This brought me together with the most beautiful activating beings throughout my whole life. Each arrived to meet me in my current evolution with a new gift of awareness and challenge to be in pure truth.

Thank God my little voice so persistently carried me from one experience of illumination to the next. Thank God she knew how to knock out the fear long enough to push me over the edge of the next cliff. Thank God she believed in me enough to invest this lifetime in merging so fully with her finite physical form.

All along, I sought the outside experience of love when all along, I was already love itself, and I was already proving it in the most authentic and deliberate ways in each moment of my life, even when I could not see it.

While the body-mind dislikes discomfort, conflict is the catalyst that creates the sparks of transformation. Just as life is created through the friction of bodies moving in physical merging, new creations, ideas, and awakenings come from the internal conflict of mind, eventually resulting in surrendered unified knowing as we hold the entire perspective as one.

The polarity is a divine creation. The pain is as beautiful as the pleasure. Both are rich and decadent in their own right, bringing gifts of evolving perceptions and awareness. Seeing this now took all judgment and anticipation away. I no longer sought the vision of what was ahead, and I no longer saw it either.

Every pathway of knowing the future was gone. Every glimpse of the potential painful endings was gone. Such peace filled me. Such clarity and fresh potential was felt, like walking around the corner in a city you'd never been, in a country you'd never traveled, in a moment you'd never lived. So present, so creative, right in the absolute zero point of the creation itself, right at the event horizon of what was next, with the pure live streaming presence of a child.

Everything I ever needed was brought to me. The perfection of everything was mind-blowing. Why would I doubt again? I would handle anything that came my way and trust that there was an immense gift and purpose in its coming.

I had every being in the universe to thank for my experience of opening to these greater truths, but Max had come in to take me to the final thread and expose the entire illusion all at once. While the ultimate truth is that Max is a real 3-D, living, breathing being, his pure essence literally extended himself through all the dimensions to find me and awaken me to my truest self.

My literal journey to Rennes Les Bains, France, in 2008, never made it into the first book. When I completed *Avatar Anatomy* and realized I had missed it, the book simply said, "It's not time." Instead of finding the perfect spot to squeeze the story in, I surrendered it and published the first book without it.

Then, in *Waking the Goddess,* as I sat allowing the alternate story to flood through my fingers, France appeared right out the mists of my memories.

In 2008, when I journeyed to this area, I was continuously met by local residents welcoming me back, even though I had never travelled there before. This happened repeatedly, until finally, at the base of the path leading to the Seat of Isis, a lovely gentleman took my hands and assured me that I had, indeed, been there before.

My time at the waterway and the magical stone chair was filled with the presence of eternal love. I rested on the larger stone, that sat deeper in the forest, and surrendered my whole heart with such peace. I could have laid there forever. I felt so full, so whole and so sensual.

The next day I journeyed to the Fountains of the Lovers for a deeply personal ceremony. This is a beautiful setting amongst trees where two streams join into one waterfall, filling pools with the clearest most sacred, delicious water.

Witnessed by four beautiful women, I walked barefoot across the flat rocks stationed amongst the water in the pools, wearing a flowing orange dress with shimmering blue sapphires around my neck. I stood with a candle in one hand as I read aloud the vows I had written upon a scroll. I read aloud the promises I was making to myself. I entered into the divine union of marriage with me. It's true. I went to France, in 2008, to offer my heart to the truest of divine unions, the one within.

These were my vows.

"I vow to walk in beauty and grace with ease and joy, being in my full power and illuminating my light with love. I vow to embody the light and allow myself to shine. I vow to experience pleasure with joy and surrender. I vow to express my authentic self and share my gifts. And in all this, I vow to invite others to join me." ~ France, September 2008

He was there the whole time. He was in the water. He was in the wind. He was in the sun and within the stones beneath my feet. He was in the leaves of the trees above me. He held my hand as I moved from the waterway to the Seat of Isis. He was in the courtyard where we sipped our tea and ate delicious meals under the beautiful tree. He was there in his full multidimensional self and the book was simply saving the experience until I could truly understand it.

Now I could see him in the higher dimensions, standing at the tree, holding the lantern and smiling. He is a being of pure-heart conviction with intention to do only good. He is the divine masculine that is waking.

Oh my God! What a gift to be in this human form on this quest to travel the full spectrum of polarity in creation and experience of life. Thank you, God! We've spanned the lows to the highs, the pain to the pleasure, and the separation to the union. All created by the illusion of one single thread split within our own spine.

And thank you, Max, beautiful cosmic Max. It is so comforting to know you breathe, and that you have been a constant in my entire existence. What depth of connection I have experienced in simply glancing into your eyes. What depth of love I have felt in wanting your deepest of happiness regardless of my placement in your life. To know such unconditional love, to feel such freedom in everything, it comes from this quest to merge with you.

Thank you for showing up so perfectly in this moment in exactly the way I needed to have this remembrance and shift in my life. You are the perfect reflection of me in my multidimensional creation. You have shown me that I am ready for true divine union. You have brought me to this embodiment of truth. I shall cherish you for eternity and bow with the most humbled gratitude in your presence. I love you absolutely and unconditionally and I see the radiance of your truest self in the reflection of my own eyes.

Chapter 27

I had no idea what being the scribe of this book meant. I had no idea I was born for these realizations. And I have no idea what is next. I have no clue where life will lead me or how I will navigate it. But all the pain feels like a memory now, or a story that I read somewhere, in a history book perhaps, a story of a time of illusion. I feel that I have woken from a dream and that I am looking upon a fertile garden that awaits immaculate seeds.

My circuits are open. The creative control panel is fresh and new. A fountain of the creative sexual Shakti energy bubbles through me unimpeded and circulates through a fountain within my own sphere. My ship is fully upgraded with a brand-new operating system. It runs on the perpetual motion of the zero point from a joystick of centered awareness. A whole new adventure of learning and navigation has begun. A whole new world is being conceived.

There is no letting go and no hanging on. I just am. I vibrate in the very core of my own spine, in a state of faith. I live in the space of every cell in my body and in the divine energy that floods within, through, and all around me.

I am aware of wholeness all at once, and I experience everything with a kind of joy that echoes out beyond me.

I no longer feel the longing, for I feel your heartbeat within my own. I feel your emotions in my cells, your thoughts as they speak to mine. I feel your warmth and your love, and I feel it all within a sea of relaxation, faith, and pure grace that needs no form. We are a gift for humanity. We are a field of truth that knows no end. How profound that we should come to resonate this way and need nothing in return.

I marvel as I realize how it has all been right in front of me the whole time, only I had no conscious awareness of it. As more and more of us become aware of our unified selves, we will see that the merging is that of spheres joining to create unions within the tapestry of the universe. Together we create the most beautiful flower of life pattern that extends forever.

It has always been this way, but our limited awareness has kept us in the linear function of time and space along a simple thread of separation and union.

Ultimately, divine union is happening within us, within the very circuitry of our own bodies, but it is also happening all around us. We are not internal OR external. We are internal AND external. So, in addition to truly going inward to love ourselves the best way we know how, why not totally love up the person we are with? Be it our child, our lover, our boss, the gas station attendant, or the annoying driver in front of us. What if we just showed up and loved them as profoundly as we could?

All the while, remembering that loving someone doesn't mean sacrificing ourselves to do it. What will love look like when we love from the wholehearted expression of not needing anything in return? Where we have looped the momentum of the polarity swing inward into the perpetual primordial union of true self? Where we love freely and unconditionally?

It's an easy trap to get into—sacrificing ourselves for another, and then resenting them or the world around us because we feel depleted or unfulfilled. Our happiness really is our own responsibility, and, at the same time, everyone is also our responsibility. We are one big connected sea of common unity.

What if we loved a person who was having trouble loving herself or himself? What could we do from a fully filled essence of being open to simply share the love all around us?

I am so grateful for all the beautiful catalysts who have reflected back to me that which I have been projecting. You are showing me a perfect mirror, so I can adjust to be more authentic and transparent in each moment. I see the depth and beauty in you, and it is my pleasure to reflect that back to you as I gaze into your eyes.

We are returning to the Garden of Eden, where Adam and Eve originally were naked—naked in their essence, not ashamed of their perceived differences and illusory shortcomings. What if we just accepted that there is nothing truly wrong with us, and we just got raw and naked in our authenticity? What if we just told the truth?

Ultimately, what are we afraid of? We are afraid of judgment. What if we didn't judge ourselves? What if we remembered that we are humans balancing polarity and doing the best we know how in every moment? Then if someone else judged us, we would just have compassion and say, "Here is an opportunity for them to see a reflection of what is inside them."

Ultimately the idea of judgment comes from the historical notion that God will punish us for our sins. If

God is the Alpha and the Omega, the beginning and the end, as stated in the Bible, then God is the unified field of oneness. God is then both the transmission and its returning echo, the projector and the screen. God is the beginning and the end, the totality of the cause and the effect.

What if the separation option of the game is simply the chance to take the beautiful gift of the Avatar body, like a curious child with a new toy on Christmas, and dismantle it so we can understand how it works? What if the lesson in this part of the game is to show us how we are cocreating our reality with the echoing pulse of God? What if being cast out of the Garden was simply a necessary move on the board game to initiate the lesson, rather than punishment as many perceive?

The separation choice shows us that our judgment of ourselves is what creates the judgment of God. What we echo out in our beliefs and attitudes is what we create. One thing Max repeated continuously throughout all of our time together was that God doesn't make mistakes. There is a reason for everything. Perhaps we could consider the value of the separation experience as having this very good purpose to exist.

Someone asked me why I was so willing to share the most intimate details of my life on the pages of a book. It is because the more naked I get in my authenticity, the more relaxed I feel. As I speak my truest truth, I feel self-compassion and forgive my prior judgment of myself.

If people get uncomfortable, then I've simply offered them an opportunity to grow from the internal conflict that has arisen within them. This is their chance to find their truest truth.

If people disagree with my points of view or methods, that is awesome. That is diversity, and that is part of the human experience of polarity. No matter what, I will feel whole and expressed because I have been as real as I know how to be in that very moment. I will feel that I have lived my purpose in showing up fully as me.

I have one friend I call a subconscious spelunker. He is excellent at spotting a contradiction in a person, and then questioning just enough to make them uncomfortable. He literally repels deep into their subconscious mind with a headlamp on and peers into what is happening. I love this guy! He can make me squirm in seconds.

Why do I love him? Because he can take me right to the edge of the cliff and offer to push me if I'll let him. I always come out more vulnerable and more authentic every time. He is not afraid of the mess. To him, it's like watching a *National Geographic* special on human behavior.

If this feels scary, ask yourself this question: how would you respond if a person in front of you simply began to sob and tell you from their heart the depth of a fear? I bet you would feel compassion, I bet your heart would open, and I bet you would be inspired by their brave example. So why not give that gift to someone else who's afraid to be exposed?

Divine union isn't just the intense connection of lovers who can't take their eyes off each other, although that is a cherished and beautiful part of it. Divine union is all of us, and because we are just one big beautiful echo, reverberating and resonating off each other, it begins with us. As within, so without.

Love yourself. Stop seeing yourself as flawed. Forgive all that no longer serves your highest evolution. Create a beautiful garden.

You are human balancing polarities. If your swing is wide, you are an adventurer. If your swing is narrow, you are a profound stabilizer. We all get to play both of those roles anyway, because they, too, are the polarity. So fun!

There is nothing to fix, nothing to even change. There is only awareness and choice in every moment and compassion for self and others, because, at the bottom of it all, there is only love, and love is the unified creative field of energy that connects us. Be grateful for this gift of life.

All people are waking, and this book applies to creative feminine energy in both men and women. The creative free flow of our sensual and sexual energy is the key to freedom within the body and liberation of the mind forms that have contracted silly beliefs and misunderstandings into our body lenses.

It is the flow of this creative, sexual energy that births absolutely every experience into our lives. Don't be ashamed of it. Let it heal you. Loop it in to nourish and clarify you. Claim it as natural. Share it as a sacred divine offering.

Question everything. If it doesn't feel comfortable, it's because you are in the process of transformation. Get excited! You are seeing a veil that is not real. Internal conflict is the rubbing together of sticks that create the spark of fire. When the fire ignites, let it flow and consume all that is false.

If tears come, cry. If it's funny, laugh. If it's anger, tone. If it's love, embrace. If it's sensual, make love. Let the energy move.

We are all ascending, and we are doing it within the body, not beyond it. Get in there. Get comfortable. Get uncomfortable. Learn your circuits. Run the energy. Shift and train your mind to love what is. Train your mind to love you, and you will inspire a world of shift around you.

I promise you that we are all on the same path, and everything that stands between you and the true divine union is melting away. Have faith. The path is lit. Trust your heart and move with courage. We are all in this together.

Max and I will be connected for eternity in a field of truth that knows no end. It will not matter what configuration our relationship takes or how often we grace each other's physical presence, or even if we ever see each other again. We are still vibrating in a cosmic orgasm that occurred at the spark of the very first light, and this echoes on and on and on into eternity.

Our field needs no physical structure to anchor its portal. Our temples are in our hearts. We just are a field of divine union, activated by our awareness, and harmonized through our own experience of illumination. The simple act of knowing this ignites the entire grid of unity. How free. How beautiful. How profound. How true.

As for humanity as a whole, what wondrous explosive creative energy will flood through our heightened awareness as we all begin to experience this NEW OS? What mind-blowing connections will we attract into our lives as we radiate our truest unconditional loving selves and have them echoed and reflected back through the eyes of another? What depths of heart will we touch? What heights of ecstasy will we reach? What truths will we know? What wondrous epic adventures await us all in this embodied bliss dimension of spherical awareness and merging?

And for me, what wondrous being will next enter my life and take me to new heights of self-discovery?

My body ripples with waves of excitement as the questions echo out beyond me, and I await their answers' return.

The illusions are gone; the concept of divine union is a given. The dream has ended. I feel whole. I feel you. I am here. I am now. This goddess is awake, and I breathe.

Oh, my beloveds, we all breathe.

Afterward ..

I am so excited to see what Book Three: *The New OS* has in store for me to experience. It is beginning to pour through my fingers and asks me to, once again, pack my suitcase and travel.

It's positioned me for full trust in the universe, making choices through my live streaming operating system, and having full faith that everything I need will come to me in its right timing and form.

I know that part of the experience required, in writing this book, will come from sharing the practices and concepts that have aided me in my own understanding. If you feel resonance to be part of that, please tune into my website, www.zeropointperspectives.com for the latest in Body Ascension Playshop offerings.

I love practices where shifts occur naturally through immersion. I look so forward to who will show up and what we teach each other.

Sat nam beautiful souls, and thank you again for your presence in my life and in my words.

Eternally grateful and loving,
~ Angela

Made in the USA
Columbia, SC
30 September 2018